Study Symbols for The Book of Ezekiel

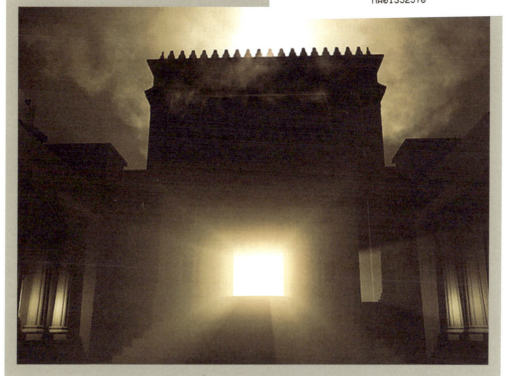

by Dr. Billye Brim

A Glorious Church Fellowship, Inc.
BILLYE BRIM MINISTRIES
PO BOX 40 | BRANSON, MO 65615
(800) 972-3447 | WWW.BILLYEBRIM.ORG

Unless otherwise indicated, all Scripture quotations are from the *King James Version* of the Bible. Public Domain.

Study Syllabus for The Book of Ezekiel
by Dr. Billye Brim
Paperback ISBN: 978-0-9742156-3-1

Cover Design and Layout by Susan Lofland

Published by
A Glorious Church Fellowship, Inc.
Billye Brim Ministries
Prayer Mountain in the Ozarks
PO Box 40
Branson, MO 65615
(417) 336-4877
www.BillyeBrim.org

Copyright 2015
All Rights Reserved.
Printed in the United States of America.

Contents

Preface	5

Section I
Foundations for Understanding The Prophet Ezekiel

Prophecy in Scripture - Its Place and Importance	7
Key to Rightyly Dividing Prophetic Scriptures	11
The Jews, The Nations, and The Church	13
Introduction to The Book of Ezekiel	19

Section II
Commentary on The Book of Ezekiel

Chapter 1	23
Chapters 2 & 3	29
Chapters 4 & 5	33
Chapters 6 & 7	35
Chapters 8, 9, 10, & 11	37
Chapters 12 - 19	45
Chapter 20	49
Chapters 21 - 23	53
Chapter 24	55
Chapter 25	57
Chapters 26, 27, 28	59
Chapters 29 - 33	63
Chapter 34	65
Chapter 35	67
Chapter 36	73
Chapter 37	83
Chapter 38 & 39	87
Chapter 40 - 48	99
Appendix	105
Sources	127

Preface

We are living in what the original Hebrew text of the Bible calls *"the end of days."* The King James Version translates the phrase as *"the latter days."* (See Appendix: Seven Days Chart of Years.)

Darkness can mean the unknown. Most of what is happening now, and will happen in the future—both short term, and long term—is unknown to the vast majority of earth's population. Therefore it falls into the realm of darkness.

The Bible declares that there is a God-given light of revelation that shines upon the unknown—illuminating the darkness of these days and the days to come. This light is written down for us, primarily in the Books of the Old Testament Prophets.

Peter, eyewitness to the Transfiguration, writes that there is a revelation even more sure than that glorious event—the prophetic written Word of God.

> For we...were eyewitnesses of His majesty.
> For He received from God the Father honour and glory, when there came such a Voice to Him from the excellent glory, This is my beloved Son, in whom I am well pleased.
> And this Voice which came from heaven we heard, when we were with Him in the holy mount.
> We have also a more sure word of prophecy; whereunto ye do well that ye take heed, as unto a light that shineth in a dark place, until the day dawn, and the day star arise.
> In your hearts knowing this first, that no prophecy of the scripture is of any private interpretation. For the prophecy came not in old time by the will of man: but holy men of God spake *as they were* moved by the Holy Ghost.
>
> —2 Peter 1:17-21

The "prophecy of the scripture" that Peter refers to is the only Scripture they knew—the Hebrew Tanach which Christians call The Old Testament.

We are advised to "take heed unto them." For they are "a light that shineth" in the dark places of what is now past to us, and of the present, and the future.

Yechezkel, Ezekiel, is one of the most enlightening of those Books of the Prophets. In it you will find brilliant light on these days and the days to come. And you will see a revelation of the Shechinah Glory you may never have seen.

—**Dr. Billye Brim**

SECTION I

Foundations for Understanding the Prophet Ezekiel

Prophecy in Scripture
Its Place and Importance

I. Prophecy

    A. Defined in Jewish Oral Law
       Talmud, Mishnah

        1. *The link between the Creator and His creatures, by means of prophecy, is one of the foundations of the creation of the world.* (Chazon Ish, Emunah &'Bitachon, ch. 6).[1]

        2. Twice as many prophets arose among the Jews as there were Israelites who left Egypt.
Only such prophecy that was needed for later generations was written down. (Megillah 14a).[2]

        3. Of these millions of Jews...the prophecies of only 48 men and 7 women have been recorded in Scriptures. Of these 55, in many cases very few of their prophecies are recorded, as little as a sentence or two in some cases.[3]
[The number applies to the Tanach]

        4. God-breathed words became the Holy Scriptures.

            2 Tim. 3:16 All scripture *is* given by inspiration of God, and *is* profitable for doctrine, for reproof, for correction, for instruction in righteousness:

        5. Peter reveals how Prophetic Scripture came and calls New Testament believers to heed what the Prophets wrote. (See Preface.)

            2 Peter 1:19-21
19 We have also ==a more sure word of prophecy;== whereunto ye do well that ye take heed, as unto a light that shineth in a dark place, until the day dawn, and the day star arise.
20 *In your hearts knowing this first, that ==no prophecy of the scripture== is of any private interpretation.

> 21 For the prophecy came not in old time by the will of man: but holy men of God spake *as they were* moved by the Holy Ghost
>
> * <u>Brim Note:</u> I have taken the liberty to move the last phrase in v.19 to v.20. There is no punctuation in the original Scriptures. In the 1980s an elderly Finnish scholar, who had done a Finnish translation of the Bible, explained to me that it should be translated thusly, since Jesus has already arisen in the believer's heart.

6. David Baron wrote: The mission of the prophets was comprehensive and many-sided; they spoke to all times, making known to the children of men the counsels of the Eternal. They spoke from the mouth of the Omniscient God, foretelling things to come; but to the current generations in which they lived they were chiefly preachers of righteousness, and their constant cry was, "Repent."[4]

B. Israel – Nation with the Prophetic Anointing

1. **Rom. 3:1** What advantage then hath the Jew? or what profit *is there* of circumcision?
Rom. 3:2 Much every way: chiefly, because that unto them were committed the oracles of God.

2. **Psa. 105:14** He suffered no man to do them wrong: yea, he reproved kings for their sakes;
Psa. 105:15 *Saying,* Touch not mine anointed, and do my prophets no harm.

   a. Sarah; Genesis 12;17; 20:18
   Rebekah, Genesis 26:11

   Psalm 105 refers to the Matriarchs of Israel, for the nation—who would speak and record the Word of God to the world—was in their wombs.

3. Jesus instructed, when asked what would be the sign of His coming and of the end of the age:
"Behold the fig tree...."
(Matthew 24:1-3; Luke 21:29.)

   Any serious study of Eschatology must include a study of Israel (the Fig Tree).

C. God has chosen that His Holy written Word be more than one-half prophecy; some say, two-thirds.

1. Many prophecies have been fulfilled.

D. God's Litmus Test for being God: *Telling the end from the beginning.*

   Isaiah 41:8,9,11,12, 22,23,26

E. By God's Design: The Jews (Israel) and His fulfilled prophecies concerning that prophetic nation are the witnesses that He is God.

   Isaiah 43:1-12
   Is. 43:1 But now thus saith the LORD that created thee, O Jacob, and he that formed thee, O Israel, Fear not: for I have redeemed thee, I have called *thee* by thy name; thou *art* mine.
   Is. 43:5 Fear not: for I *am* with thee: I will bring thy seed from the east, and gather thee from the west;
   Is. 43:6 I will say to the north, Give up; and to the south, Keep not back: bring my sons from far, and my daughters from the ends of the earth;
   Is. 43:7 *Even* every one that is called by my name: for I have created him for my glory, I have formed him; yea, I have made him.
   Is. 43:8 Bring forth the blind people that have eyes, and the deaf that have ears.
   Is. 43:9 Let all the nations be gathered together, and let the people be assembled: who among them can declare this, and shew us former things? let them bring forth their witnesses, that they may be justified: or let them hear, and say, *It is* truth.
   Is. 43:10 Ye *are* my witnesses, saith the LORD, and my servant whom I have chosen: that ye may know and believe me, and understand that I *am* he: before me there was no God formed, neither shall there be after me.
   Is. 43:11 I, *even* I, *am* the LORD; and beside me *there is* no saviour.
   Is. 43:12 I have declared, and have saved, and I have shewed, when *there* was no strange *god* among you: therefore ye *are* my witnesses, saith the LORD, that I *am* God.

   Isaiah 44:6,7,8
   Is. 44:6 Thus saith the LORD the King of Israel, and his redeemer the LORD of hosts; I *am* the first, and I *am* the last; and beside me *there is* no God.
   Is. 44:7 And who, as I, shall call, and shall declare it, and set it in order for me, since I appointed the ancient people? and the things that are coming, and shall come, let them shew unto them.
   Is. 44:8 Fear ye not, neither be afraid: have not I told thee from that time, and have declared *it*? *ye are* even my witnesses. Is there a God beside me? yea, *there is* no God; I know not *any*.

F. Prophetic understanding: spiritual weapon of the Army of the Lord

   1. One of His Names is *Yaweh Sabaoth,* Jehovah of hosts, or armies. David Baron defines that special name:

"Jehovah of hosts...Lord of all things, at whose call all created forces must marshal themselves as if for war."[5]

2. Attribute of the Army of the LORD

> **1 Chr. 12:22** For at *that* time day by day there came to David to help him, until *it was* a great host, like the host of God.
> **1 Chr. 12:23** And these *are* the numbers of the bands *that were* ready armed to the war, *and* came to David to Hebron, to turn the kingdom of Saul to him, according to the word of the LORD...
>
> **1 Chr. 12:32** And of the children of Issachar, *which were men* that ==had understanding of the times, to know what Israel ought to do;== the heads of them *were* two hundred; and all their brethren *were* at their commandment...
> **1 Chr. 12:38** All these men of war, that could keep rank, came with a perfect heart to Hebron, to make David king over all Israel: and all the rest also of Israel *were* of one heart to make David king.

Brim Note: First Chronicles 12 describes God's view of the attributes of the army that came to make David king. It typifies the army of the Lord in *the End of Days* and the same attributes which army should possess before the coming of The King of Kings.

3. Light from the Prophets is a huge part of one's stability in *the End of Days.*

> **Is. 33:6** And wisdom and knowledge shall be the stability of thy times,

---

1. *Trei Asar, The Twelve Prophets, Vol. 1: Hosea, Joel, Amos, Obadiah,* Editors Rabbi Nosson Scherman/Rabbi Meir Zlotowitz, ArtScrolls Tanach Series, Overview by Rabbi Joseph Elias, Mesorah Publications, ltd, Brooklyn, NY, xvii.
2. Ibid., xviii.
3. Ibid.
4. ZECHARIAH, *A Commentary on his Visions and Prophecies,* David Baron, Kregel Publications, Grand Rapids, MI, 11.
5. Ibid.

SECTION I

Foundations for Understanding the Prophet Ezekiel

Key to Rightly Dividing Prophetic Sciptures
Understanding the Three Groups of People

I. Rightly Dividing the Word

> **2 Tim. 2:15** Study to shew thyself approved unto God, a workman that needeth not to be ashamed, rightly dividing the word of truth.

   A. The Bible is the Word of Truth.
   It must be rightly divided.
   Since it can be rightly divided, it can also be wrongly divided.
   Error in interpretation comes from a wrong division of the Scripture.
   For example: Assigning a verse to the church which really refers to the Jews or the Nations. This is why some erroneously teach that the church will go through the tribulation period on earth.

II. Three Groups of People

   There are three people groups to or about whom prophetic scriptures speak.
   A Scripture can refer to any one of the three; or, to more than one.
   The Scripture is plain as to whom it refers.

   A. The Jews
   The Nations
   The Church

   > **1 Cor. 10:32** Give none offence, neither to the Jews, nor to the Gentiles (Nations), nor to the church of God:

   Some English translations of this verse translate Greeks rather than Gentiles. This is because the Gentile world had been Hellenized (or Greekilized) after the conquests of Alexandar the Great.
   The biblical meaning is "nations."
   Goyim in the Hebrew of Genesis Chapter Ten where the Gentile nations are introduced. Law of first mention.

III. Some Rules of Bible Interpretation;
Rightly Dividing the Word of God.

1. Read the Scripture in context.

2. Be sure it harmonizes with all God's Word on the matter.

    > Do not lift scriptures out of context, or out of the entirety of the Word of God, on the matter. This is the meaning of the following verse:
    >
    > **2 Pet. 1:20** Knowing this first, that no prophecy of the scripture is of any **private interpretation.**

3. Know *who* is speaking.

4. Know *to whom* a Scripture is speaking.

    A Scripture may be speaking to:

    a. An individual

    b. A group.

        1) Jews
        2) Nations (Hebrew: *Goyim*)
        3) The Church

SECTION I

Foundations for Understanding the Prophet Ezekiel

The Jews, The Nations, and The Church

1 Cor. 10:32 Give none offence, neither to the Jews, nor to the Gentiles, nor to the church of God:

The three primary groups of peoples to or about whom Scripture is written are:

1. The Jews

2. The Nations
    (O.T. Hebrew: *Goyim,* meaning nations.)
    (Greek N.T. translates Gentiles, or Greeks.)

3. The Church
    (Greek: *Ekklesia,* assembly.)
    "The Greek word, *ekklesia* means *assembly,* or a gathering of called-out ones."

E. W. Bullinger, *The Companion Bible,* Appendix 186.
"The Greek word, *ekklesia* means *assembly,* or a gathering of called out ones."

Dr. Kenneth E. Hagin, *Marriage, Divorce, and Remarriage,* Page 18.
"When I first got saved and started in the ministry, I heard someone give this simple rule of Bible interpretation, and it registered on me. In studying the Bible, always ask yourself: 'Who's doing the speaking?' 'What are they speaking about?' 'And to whom are they speaking?'

"It's very easy to take some of the things that God said and say, 'Well, now, God is saying this.' But you have to look at whom God was talking to. Sometimes he was speaking to the Jews; and what He said didn't even apply to anyone else...

"...there are three classes of people addressed in the Word of God: 1) the Jews, God's covenant people; 2) the Church, God's own family; and 3) the Gentiles...(everyone who's not either in the Church or a Jew)."[1]

Brim Note: The order of the groups in 1 Corinthians 10:32 is: The Jews, the Gentiles, the Church of God. However, the order of their mention in the Word of God is: The Nations, the Jews (Israel), the Church (The Body of Christ).

In the Old Testament there are only two groups: The Nations, and the Jews (Israel.) We shall look at the Nations first, as they are the first of the groups to exist.

I. **The Nations**

   A. <u>First Mention</u>

   The first of the three groups introduced in Scripture is the *Goyim* (Nations).
   By the law of first mention, the biblical account of the roots of this group is of utmost and continuing importance.

   Before the flood of Genesis 7, God saw "the wickedness of man was great" (Gen. 6:5). Love brought the flood. Only one man and his family knew God. If Love (God) had delayed judgment, knowledge of God could have disappeared from the earth. Eight people were saved: Noah and his wife, their three sons and their wives.

   After the flood, the Bible introduces the nations *(goyim)* in the progeny of Noah's three sons: Shem, Ham, and Japheth.

   It is in the 10th chapter of Genesis that we first see the word *goyim* (nations). There, seventy foundational nations are introduced.
   (To arrive at 70, do not count Noah's three sons, nor the Philistines of verse 14. See chart in Appendix.)

   B. <u>God's Will and Instructions For After the Flood</u>

   > **Gen. 9:1** And God blessed Noah and his sons, and said unto them, Be fruitful, and multiply, and replenish the earth.

   C. <u>The Rebellion of the *Goyim* (Nations)</u>

   God commanded them what to do when the waters receded. To replenish (fill) the earth, they would have had to move through the earth, but 340 years after the flood they still were together in one place. They were concentrated in what became known in the 20th Century as Iraq. In the Bible, *Shinar* is Babylon:

   > **Gen. 11:1** And the whole earth was of one language, and of one speech.
   > **Gen. 11:2** And it came to pass, as they journeyed from the east, that they found a plain in the land of Shinar; and they dwelt there.
   > **Gen. 11:3** And they said one to another, Go to, let us make brick, and burn them throughly. And they had brick for stone, and slime had they for morter.
   > **Gen. 11:4** And they said, Go to, let us build us a city and a tower, whose top *may reach* unto heaven; and let us make us a name, ==lest we be scattered abroad upon the face of the whole earth.==

Open rebellion against the commandment of God.

> **Gen. 11:5** And the LORD came down to see the city and the tower, which the children of men builded.
> **Gen. 11:6** And the LORD said, Behold, the people *is* one, and they have all one language; and this they begin to do: and now nothing will be restrained from them, which they have imagined to do.
> **Gen. 11:7** Go to, let us go down, and there confound their language, that they may not understand one another's speech.
> **Gen. 11:8** So the LORD scattered them abroad from thence upon the face of all the earth: and they left off to build the city.
> **Gen. 11:9** Therefore is the name of it called Babel; because the LORD did there confound the language of all the earth: and from thence did the LORD scatter them abroad upon the face of all the earth.

D. Instigators of the Rebellion

Satan means *adversary*. He is the ancient adversary of God, and the author of confusion. Satan certainly was behind the rebellion of the nations. The human instrument he used was Nimrod.

> **Gen. 10:8** And Cush begat Nimrod: he began to be a mighty one in the earth.
> **Gen. 10:9** He was a mighty hunter before the LORD: wherefore it is said, Even as Nimrod the mighty hunter before the LORD.
> **Gen. 10:10** And the beginning of his kingdom was Babel, and Erech, and Accad, and Calneh, in the land of Shinar.
>
> <u>*The Stone Edition of the Chumash*, page 47</u>
> Before Nimrod there were neither wars nor reigning monarchs. He subjugated the Babylonians until they crowned him (v.10), after which he went to Assyria and built great cities (Radak; Ramban). The Torah calls him a mighty hunter, which Rashi and most commentators interpret figuratively: Nimrod ensnared men with his words and incited them to rebel against God (R. Hirsch). His first conquest, which laid the basis for his subsequent empire building was Babel, which became the center of Nebuchadnezzar's Babylonian Empire. It was one of the greatest cities of the ancient world.[2]

With this rebellion began the Babylonian System—and all things Babylon.
Kenneth Copeland, in teaching about the Babylonian System called it, "Man's attempt to meet his own needs without God."

II. The Jews, The Separated Nation

The Jews are the second group of peoples to be introduced in God's Word.

Only two of the three groups appear in the Old Testament:
The Jews and the Nations.

==Not willing that the nations perish, God initiated the plan He'd designed long before its need manifested.== He separated a nation unto Himself for His use. A Holy Nation. With a Holy Call. He would use the separated nation to reveal Himself to the rebellious nations.

> **Gen. 12:1** Now the LORD had said unto Abram, Get thee out of thy country, and from thy kindred, and from thy father's house, unto a land that I will shew thee:
> **Gen. 12:2** And I will make of thee a great nation, and I will bless thee, and make thy name great; and thou shalt be a blessing:
> **Gen. 12:3** And I will bless them that bless thee, and curse him that curseth thee: and in thee shall all families of the earth be blessed. (KJV)

==God called a man who would live by faith t==o be the Patriarch of a "great nation" separated, holy unto God.

He rewarded Abraham, the first Jew, and his natural seed by promising them a Land. And He proclaimed a blessing upon them.

God promised to personally bless those who bless them.
God promised to personally curse him who curses them.

In many ways, the families of the earth are blessed in Abraham and his seed.
Foremost in the Seed Who is the Messiah.
But, also, in the Millennium and the ages to follow, the blessings of the earth and the sheep nations are tied up in the blessings of Israel.

Israel's Purpose and Call

> ==The call that Israel as a nation has upon it is: To reveal God to the nations.==

> First, to the rebellious nations of Genesis 11, and subsequently to their progeny.

> In Romans 9, 10, and 11—a revelation of "the mystery of Israel" to the church—the Lord declares that He has not withdrawn that call.

>> **Rom. 11:25** For I would not, brethren, that ye should be ignorant of this mystery, lest ye should be wise in your own conceits; that blindness in part is happened to Israel, until the fulness of the Gentiles be come in.
>> **Rom. 11:26** And so all Israel shall be saved: as it is written,

There shall come out of Sion the Deliverer, and shall turn away ungodliness from Jacob:
Rom. 11:27 For this *is* my covenant unto them, when I shall take away their sins.
Rom. 11:28 As concerning the gospel, *they are* enemies for your sakes: but as touching the election, *they are* beloved for the fathers' sakes.
Rom. 11:29 For the gifts and calling of God *are* without repentance. (KJV)

(We often use verse 29 to show that if one is called by God into a certain office, God never repents, or changes His mind, regarding the call. And it is all right to do that, for this verse shows the character of God. However, the verse is not to be removed from its first meaning, that God does not repent of His call upon Israel.)

Plan "A"

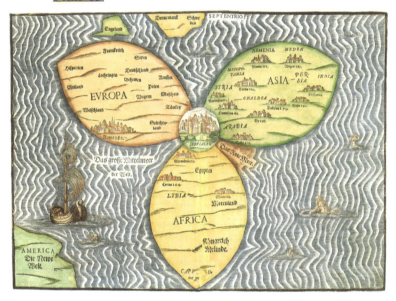

God's Plan "A" was for Israel to reveal God to the nations by living in the Promised Land and demonstrating Jehovah God and His blessings upon them there. The Ancient Map here and in the Appendix shows the strategic location of that Land.

Read all of Deuteronomy 28:1-14.

Deut. 28:10 And all people of the earth shall see that thou art called by the name of the LORD; and they shall be afraid of thee.
Deut. 28:11 And the LORD shall make thee plenteous in goods, in the fruit of thy body, and in the fruit of thy cattle, and in the fruit of thy ground, in the land which the LORD sware unto thy fathers to give thee...
Deut. 28:14 And thou shalt not go aside from any of the words which I command thee this day, *to* the right hand, or *to* the left, to go after other gods to serve them. (KJV)

Israel's strategic location as a land bridge between three continents made it an easier route for caravans and armies. When they traveled through, the nations were to see a people who worshiped the One True God who blessed them. All the blessings of Deuteronomy 28 were material, physical, and financial. They could be seen. Thus the Chosen People—chosen to reveal God—could fulfill their calling.

Plan "B"

> **Deut. 28:64** And the LORD shall scatter thee among all people, from the one end of the earth even unto the other...

If Israel did not hearken to the commandments of God in obedience, He would scatter them from one end of earth to the other. And then in the "end of days," He promised to gather them back to their Promised Land. In the evident keeping of His Word to bring them home, the nations would be provided a revelation of God.

God Prophesied Through Moses What Would Happen

> **Deut. 30:1** And it shall come to pass, when all these things are come upon thee, the blessing and the curse, which I have set before thee, and thou shalt call them to mind among all the nations, whither Jehovah thy God hath driven thee,
> **Deut. 30:2** and shalt return unto Jehovah thy God, and shalt obey his voice according to all that I command thee this day, thou and thy children, with all thy heart, and with all thy soul;
> **Deut. 30:3** that then Jehovah thy God will 1turn thy captivity, and have compassion upon thee, and will return and gather thee from all the peoples, whither Jehovah thy God hath scattered thee.
> **Deut. 30:4** If *any of* thine outcasts be in the uttermost parts of heaven, from thence will Jehovah thy God gather thee, and from thence will he fetch thee:
> **Deut. 30:5** and Jehovah thy God will bring thee into the land which thy fathers possessed, and thou shalt possess it; and he will do thee good, and multiply thee above thy fathers.
> **Deut. 30:6** And Jehovah thy God will circumcise thy heart, and the heart of thy seed, to love Jehovah thy God with all thy heart, and with all thy soul, that thou mayest live.
> **Deut. 30:7** And Jehovah thy God will put all these curses upon thine enemies, and on them that hate thee, that persecuted thee.
> **Deut. 30:8** And thou shalt return and obey the voice of Jehovah, and do all his commandments which I command thee this day.
> **Deut. 30:9** And Jehovah thy God will make thee plenteous in all the work of thy hand, in the fruit of thy body, and in the fruit of thy cattle, and in the fruit of thy ground, for good: for Jehovah will again rejoice over thee for good, as he rejoiced over thy fathers;... (ASV)

The Scattering and The Ingathering are dealt with in most of the O.T. Prophets.

---

1. *Marriage Divorce & Remarriage*, Dr. Kenneth E. Hagin, Kenneth Hagin Ministries, Tulsa, OK, page 18.
2. *The Chumash, The Stone Edition,* ArtScroll Series, Mesorah Publicatons, Ltd, Brooklyn, NY, page 47.

SECTION I

Foundations for Understanding the Prophet Ezekiel

An Important Introduction to The Book of Ezekiel

God did not allow Moses to go into the Promised Land. But before Israel was to enter the Land, Moses prophesied God's dealings with Israel: The Scattering. The Ingathering. The Restoration. And the Redemption. I have quoted Moses' telling prophecy here as translated from the Hebrew to English by Hebrew scholars and speakers.

> **Deuteronomy 30:1-10** (*The Tanach, The Stone Edition, ArtScrolls Series*)
> It will be that when all these things come upon you — the blessing and the curse that I have presented before you — then you will take it to your heart among all the nations where HASHEM [The Name], your God, has dispersed you; and you will return unto HASHEM, your God, and listen to His voice, according to everything that I command you today, you and your children, with all your heart and all your soul. Then Hashem, your God, will bring back your captivity and have mercy upon you, and He will return and gather you in from all the peoples to which HASHEM, your God, has scattered you. If your dispersed will be at the ends of heaven, from there HASHEM, your God, will gather you in and from there I will take you. HASHEM, your God will bring you to the Land that your forefathers possessed and you shall possess it; He will do good to you and make you more numerous than your forefathers. HASHEM, your God, will circumcise your heart and the heart of your offspring, to love HASHEM, your God, with all your heart and with all your soul, that you may live.
>
> HASHEM, your God, will place all these imprecations upon your enemies and those who hate you, who pursued you. You shall return and listen to the voice of HASHEM, and perform all His commandments that I command you today. HASHEM will make you abundant in all your handiwork — in the fruit of your womb, the fruit of your animals, and the fruit of your Land — for good, when HASHEM will return to rejoice over you for good, as He rejoiced over your forefathers, when you listen to the voice of HASHEM, your God, to observe His commandments and His decrees, that are written in this Book of the Torah, when you shall return to HASHEM, your God, with all your heart and all your soul.[1]

The following note to this passage in *The Chumash, the Stone Edition* is quite meaningful — both for when Moses uttered it, and for the ministry of the Prophet Ezekiel to the Nation of Israel in its first dispersion, its first scattering:

> **1-10. The eventual repentance and redemption.** After the fearsome warnings of what will befall the nation when it is disloyal to God, the Torah turns to the eventual benevolence that God will shower upon His people when they repent. Ramban notes that these promises have not been fulfilled as yet; they

will come about in the Messianic era. This passage is, in effect, a commandment to repent, but it is phrased not in the imperative form but in the ordinary future tense, because God wanted it to be an assurance to beleaguered Jews that sooner or later they will repent and be redeemed.[2]

Isaiah, Jeremiah, Ezekiel, and Daniel were the prophets of Israel's first exile — the carrying off into Babylon, and the destruction of the First Temple.

A Message of Hope to Israel

Ezekiel, like Daniel, was carried off to Babylon before the Temple was destroyed. His prophesies in Babylon that the Temple would be destroyed made him unpopular with the captives. But then, a runner came from Jerusalem with the terrible news that the Temple had been burned by Nebuchadnezzar's forces. After that, Ezekiel was exalted in their eyes.

My! How terrible they must have felt. The Temple was their connection to God. The Temple was what made them a people different from all others. For all they knew it was all over.

Indeed the Prophet Ezekiel made dire warnings, and descriptions of Israel's dark sins. But Ezekiel was also a priest, and his ministry was priestly in consolation. The Lord gave him translations and visions that prophesied of the promised redemption. He prophesied the end of days return to their Land that we are witnessing now. He foresaw in detail the Millennial Temple, the division of the Land again to the returned Tribes of Israel. The Book ends with the wonderful proclamation that the Glory will be over earthly Jerusalem when its very name shall be *Jehovah Shammah*, The LORD is There.

> **Ezek. 48:35** ...and the name of the city from *that* day *shall be,* The LORD *is* there. (KJV)

✷ The Departure and Return of the Glory

An amazing detail of this Book is one I'd never seen until I studied the ArtScroll commentaries. And yet, it is very plain in the Book itself if you just know what to look for. I just needed those who have spoken Hebrew and studied this Book for centuries to point it out.

And that is: The Departure and The Return of the Shechinah Glory.
The Chariot, Hebrew speakers call it the *Merkivah,* came to escort the Glory from the Temple. The Book describes the stations of the departure. How the Glory lifted from between the Cherabim, went out into the court, over the threshold, and then across to the Mount of Olives where it ascended into Heaven.

The Glory had to depart. For if the Glory had remained over the mercy seat, the Babylonians would never have been able to burn the Temple.

After the Glory departed, the Temple was just a building. No longer was it filled with the Glorious Presence.

The *Shechinah* Glory, as manifested in a cloud over the Mercy Seat, was never in the Second Temple.

The return of the *Shechinah* to the Millennial Temple is prophesied in this amazing Book.

> <u>*The Book of Yechezkel, An Overview*</u> <u>by Rabbi Moshe Eisemann and Rabbi Nosson Scherman</u>
>
> ...So intense was the holiness of the Shechinah, God's Presence, as it rested in a cloud upon the Tabernacle that even Moses feared to enter (Exodus 40:34-35), and so total was its presence on the Temple that the priests could not enter (I Kings 8:11). But God's Shechinah rests ultimately on His people, not on their architecture. His purpose is Man, not man's temples. So, when Israel descended from...spiritual grandeur to the earthly depths of lust and iniquity, the Shechinah ascended from Israel's Temple which had become no more than a shell — beautiful but empty — and returned to the heavens....
>
> It was the lot of Yechezkel to witness the tragedy...the departure of the Shechinah.... In ten agonizing stages, the Shechinah slowly withdrew from the Holy City and the Holy Temple, leaving them naked to the onslaught of Nebuchadnezzar.... All this Yechezkel saw....
>
> But Yechezkel's visions were not all bleak. He was more than the prophet of destruction... he saw the future, the glorious future when the Temple...eternal... would stand enveloped in a glory that would eclipse all which had gone before. Yechezkel had suffered the...torment of hearing the angels describe God's withdrawal from the Temple saying, *"Blessed is the glory of God [as He departs] 'from' His place* (3:12). He would exult with another vision as God transported him to Eretz Yisreal, and set him down on a high mountain overlooking Jerusalem (40:2).... Yechezkel would see the glory of God borne on a chariot that was not drawing away from Zion — but was returning to it, never again to depart:
>
>> *And the glory of God was coming to the House by way of the gate which faced eastward (43:4).*[3]

<u>Brim Note:</u> The Chariot of God (*Merkavah*) was sent to escort the *Shechinah*. Consider this opening to the First Chapter of Ezekiel from the *ArtScrolls*:

> *Some five years after the arrival in Babylon, of the first wave of exiles who had been led into captivity by Nebuchadnezzar's hordes. Yechezkel ben Buzi, the priest was granted a prophecy. As he stood on the banks of the river Kevar 'the heavens were opened' and he was shown 'the visions of God.'*
> *These 'visions' are known in Talmudic literature as Merkavah [lit. 'Chariot', or, Ma'aseh Merkavah, [lit. 'the Work,' or 'the Account' of the Chariot]*[4].

1. *The Tanach, The Stone Edition,* The ArtScroll Series, Mesorah Publications, Ltd., Brooklyn, NY, page 501.
2. *The Chumash, The Stone Edition,* ArtScroll, Mesorah, Publications, Ltd., page 1091.
3. *Yechezel, The Book of Ezekiel,* General Editors: Rabbi Nosson Scherman/Rabbi Meir Zlotowitz, Mesorah Publications, Ltd., Brooklyn, NY, pages xx, xxi.
4. Ibid. Page 69.

SECTION II

Commentary on The Book of Ezekiel

Ezekiel Chapter 1

Ezekiel 1:1

A. The Prophet in exile with the people of Israel in Babylon.
(Named The State of Iraq in 1920).

B. In exile, and yet, "the heavens are opened, and he sees visions of God."

The Numerical Bible:
"...the heavens are opened and there are 'visions of God.'
Whatever the message that may be given, the first thing for the prophet's soul is that there are 'visions of God.'
With God coming in, how everything changes, even though nothing may be changed! For there is no desolation like the absence of God; and there is nothing to lack with His presence realized. Thus the end is, as it were, seen from the beginning."[1]

Yechezel, ArtScrolls
Some five years after the arrival in Babylon, of the first wave of exiles who had been led into captivity by Nebuchadnezzar's hordes. Yechezkel ben Buzi, the priest was granted a prophecy. As he stood on the banks of the river Kevar 'the heavens were opened' and he was shown 'the visions of God.'
These 'visions' are known in Talmudic literature as Merkavah [lit. 'Chariot', or, Ma'aseh Merkavah, [lit. 'the Work,' or 'the Account' of the Chariot].[2]

Ezekiel 1:2, 3

A. "The hand of the LORD was upon me."

    1. Characteristic expression, used repeatedly through the Book.

    2. "The Hand of the Lord" is the Spirit of God.

        2 Pet. 1:21 For the prophecy came not in old time by the will of man: but holy men of God spake *as they were* moved by the Holy Ghost

Ezekiel 1:4, 5 (KJV)
Ezek. 1:4 And I looked, and, behold, a whirlwind came out of the north, a great cloud, and a fire infolding itself, and a brightness *was* about it, and out of the midst thereof as the colour of amber, out of the midst of the fire.

Ezek. 1:5 Also out of the midst thereof *came* the likeness of four living creatures.

Ezekiel 1:4,5 (*Yechezkel*, Art Scrolls)
4 Then I looked and behold! a stormy wind was coming from the north, a great cloud with flashing fire and a brilliance surrounding it; and from its midst came a semblance of Chasmal from the midst of the fire; 5 and from its midst, a semblance of four Chayos. This was their appearance: they had the semblance of a man; and four faces for each, and four wings for each of them...

A. A stormwind—a whirlwind (King James)

- Whirlwind often used in Scripture to describe God's coming in judgment. (Isaiah 66:15, Jer. 25:32)

- Whirlwind often associated with the chariots of God.

    2 Kings 2:11 (KJV)
    And it came to pass, as they still went on, and talked, that, behold *there appeared* a chariot of fire, and horses of fire, and parted them both asunder; and Elijah went up by a whirlwind into heaven.

B. Ezekiel's Vision of the Chariot of God

www.Chabad.ORG
Ezekiel's Vision of the "Chariot" (429 BCE)
On the 5th of Tammuz of the year 3332 from creation (429 BCE), Ezekiel, the only one of the Prophets to prophesy outside of the Holy Land, beheld a vision of the Divine "Chariot"...

Brim Note re the *Wikipedia* Entry that Follows:
This is by no means to be taken as exact truth — for this vision is beyond the scope of man's definition. But perhaps it does present a visual aid of sorts. As Brother Hagin wisely counseled, we can eat the hay, and leave the sticks.

Wikipedia, The Free Encylopedia [On Line]:
Ezekiel's vision of the chariot
According to the verses in Ezekiel and its attendant commentaries, his vision consists of a chariot made of many heavenly beings driven by the "Likeness of a Man." The base structure of the chariot is composed of four beings. These beings are called the "living creatures" (Hebrew: חיות *hayyot* or *khayyot*). The bodies of the creatures are "like that of a human being", but each of them has four faces, corresponding to the four directions the chariot can go (East, South, North, and West). The faces are that of a man, a lion, an ox, and an eagle. Since there are four angels and each has four faces, there are a total of sixteen faces. Each "*Hayyot*" angel also has four wings. Two of these wings spread across the length of the chariot and connect with the wings of the angel on the other side. This creates a sort of 'box' of wings that forms the perimeter of the chariot. With the remaining two wings, each angel covers its own body. Below, but not attached to, the feet of the "*Hayyot*" angels are other

angels that are shaped like wheels. These wheel angels, which are described as "a wheel inside of a wheel", are called "*Ophanim*" אופנים (lit. wheels, cycles or ways). These wheels are not directly under the chariot but are nearby and along its perimeter. The angel with the face of the man is always on the east side and looks up at the "Likeness of a Man" that drives the chariot. The "Likeness of a Man" sits on a throne made of sapphire.

1. **Chasmal** (See ArtScrolls translation above.)

    ArtScrolls
    "The mysterious significance of this word is laden with esoteric connotation. It is a pure example of prophetic idiom, and beyond the realm of comprehension.... It is the purest form of smokeless fire that the human senses can perceive...."

    Numerical Bible (Samuel Rideout)
    "The word *hashmal* in the original is translated *electron* in the Septuagint, or *amber,* as in the KJV.... It is glory in judgment that is displayed."

    John G. Lake
    "The Presence (the Glory) of God is as destructive of evil as it is constructive of good."

    Numerical Bible
    "a great cloud, and a fire infolding itself, and a brightness about it..."
    This fire is not pure wrath; it is rather, as a symbol, the holiness of God of which it speaks, a consuming fire indeed, therefore, to iniquity, but judgment is not its essence, not what it seeks or delights in, but what is necessitated by the perfection of God Himself. The first thing indeed is that in the form of judgment, God it is who is enwrapping Himself.

2. **Chayot** (Chayos, Hayyot)

    a. Living creatures.

    b. The first woman's Hebrew name was *Chaya,* meaning *living.*

    The Numerical Bible:
    It is not a likeness of God that they present; and all likeness of Him is expressly forbidden. They are creatures of His—no more; in His hand, obedient to His will, and used for His purposes; in fact, as we shall see, instruments of His government; in Revelation (Chapter 4) seen in the midst of and around the Throne; here underneath it, for here the view is from earth, and there in heaven. They have in general the likeness of a man, but their feet are like the feet of an ox "upright" and not extended as is man's foot. They sparkle giving the look of glowing brass, reminding us once more of Revelation, but there of Him who

appears to John, and who is the Lord Himself (Revelation 1:15). A higher Spirit than that of the living creature itself in fact guided and governed all.

Ezekiel 1:19-21

Yechezkel 1:19-21
As the *Chayos* move the *Ofanim* move by them and as the *Chayos* were lifted from upon the surface, the *Ofanim* were lifted, wherever the spirit chose to go they went; there the spirit chose to go; the *Ofanim* were lifted opposite them for the spirit of the *Chayah* was in the *Ofanim*. When they moved they moved; and when they halted, they halted….

    A.   *Ofanim* = wheels

    B.   ArtScroll, page 84
In whatever direction the Will of God, Who was—if one may so express it—riding thereon [i.e. the *Merkavah*], wished to go, they went; for it was also the will of the *Chayos* to go there and thus they moved only as intended by God. (Metzudas David).

Ezekiel 1:25-28 (KJV)
Ezek. 1:25 And there was a voice from the firmament that *was* over their heads, when they stood, *and* had let down their wings.
Ezek. 1:26 And above the firmament that *was* over their heads *was* the likeness of a throne, as the appearance of a sapphire stone: and upon the likeness of the throne *was* the likeness as the appearance of a man above upon it.
Ezek. 1:27 And I saw as the colour of amber, as the appearance of fire round about within it, from the appearance of his loins even upward, and from the appearance of his loins even downward, I saw as it were the appearance of fire, and it had brightness round about.
Ezek. 1:28 As the appearance of the bow that is in the cloud in the day of rain, so *was* the appearance of the brightness round about. This *was* the appearance of the likeness of the glory of the LORD. And when I *saw it*, I fell upon my face, and I heard a voice of one that spake.

Amplified Bible
Ezek. 1:25 And there was a voice above the firmament that was over their heads; when they stood, they let down their wings.
Ezek. 1:26 And above the firmament that was over their heads was the likeness of a throne in appearance like a sapphire stone, and seated above the likeness of a throne was a likeness with the appearance of a Man.
Ezek. 1:27 From what had the appearance of His waist upward, I saw a lustre as it were glowing metal with the appearance of fire enclosed round about within it; and from the appearance of His waist downward, I saw as it were the appearance of fire, and there was brightness [of a halo] round about Him.
Ezek. 1:28 Like the appearance of the bow that is in the cloud on the day of rain, so was the appearance of the brightness round about. This was the appearance of the

likeness of the glory of the Lord. And when I saw it, I fell upon my face and I heard a voice of One speaking.

Yechezkel, ArtScrolls

25 So there was a sound from above the expanse which was upon their heads; when they halt, they release their wings. 26 And above the expanse which was above their heads was like the appearance of sapphire stone in the likeness of a throne; and upon the likeness of the throne a likeness like the appearance of a man upon it from above. 27 And I saw a semblance of ==Chashmal== like the appearance of fire within it all around from the appearance of his loins and upward; and from the appearance of his loins and downward I saw as if the appearance of fire, and it had brilliance all around. 28 Like the appearance of the bow which shall be upon the cloud on a rainy day, so was the appearance of the brilliance all around. That was the appearance of the semblance of the glory of HASHEM!

    When I saw this, I threw myself upon my face and I heard a voice speaking.

---

[1]. *The Numerical Bible,* Loizeaux Brothers, Neptune, N.J.

[2]. *Yechezel, The Book of Ezekiel,* General Editors: Rabbi Nosson Scherman/Rabbi Meir Zlotowitz, ArtScroll Tanach Series, Mesorah Publications, Ltd., Brooklyn, NY, Page 69.

SECTION II

Commentary on The Book of Ezekiel

Ezekiel Chapters 2 and 3

Ezek. 2:1 And he said unto me, Son of man [*Ben Adam*], stand upon thy feet, and I will speak unto thee.
Ezek. 2:2 And the spirit entered into me when he spake unto me, and set me upon my feet, that I heard him that spake unto me.
Ezek. 2:3 And he said unto me, Son of man [*Ben Adam*], I send thee to the children of Israel, to a rebellious nation that hath rebelled against me: they and their fathers have transgressed against me, *even* unto this very day.
Ezek. 2:4 For *they are* impudent children and stiffhearted. I do send thee unto them; and thou shalt say unto them, Thus saith the Lord GOD.
Ezek. 2:5 And they, whether they will hear, or whether they will forbear, (for they *are* a rebellious house,) yet shall know that there hath been a prophet among them.

A. *Yechezkel* means "God Strengthens." It is used only twice in the entire Book, and nowhere else in the Old Testament.

B. *Ben Adam*, Son of man, is used 90 times in this Book, and is how God addresses the Prophet.

The Ezekiel Tablets
And My Personal Experience With Them

Dr. David Allen Lewis, Assemblies of God, well-respected and outstanding teacher of prophecy, was a mentor of mine. He said of me, "You are more like me in my understanding and teaching of prophecy than anyone else." What a God-sent blessing he was to my life.

He introduced me to "The Amazing Ezekiel Tablets." (See his article by that name in the Appendices Section of this Syllabus.)

He was convinced that these stone tablets, stolen from the grave of the Prophet Ezekiel, were the original of the Book.

Dr. Lewis was ill before he passed away in 2007, and he charged me not to let go of the Ezekiel Tablets. Soon after, in Israel, I tried to make contact with "the expert" on the stones, Dr. Yehuda Oppenheim. But at first, he refused to see me. When he did at last agree and came to meet me in Jerusalem, I soon knew I was in the presence of one of the most intelligent human beings I'd ever met. A former junior chess champion, he used chess to teach specially chosen young Israelis how to think.

Several times, in Israel, I worked with this genius as we researched and dug into the Ezekiel Tablets.

Dr. Oppenheim studied the opening texts as they appear on the stone. They are almost identical with the Hebrew text we have of today. However, there are a few slight differences. One of those slight differences appears in verse 5. The past tense is not used on the tablets. Rather than saying, "there hath been a prophet among them," it is present indicating "there is a prophet among them." Thus indicating that the tablets were created by the Prophet or his scribe in his lifetime.

These tablets were stolen by thieves from Ezekiel's Tomb. Dr. Oppenheim uncovered the true story of the Tablets that would rival Indiana Jones and the Raiders of the Lost Ark. Please see in the Appendix Section of this Syllabus, excerpts from the book, *Mother of the Pound: Memoirs on the Life and History of the Iraqi Jews* by David Kazzaz. In these excerpts you will see how the Tomb of Ezekiel in Iraq became a kind of "substitution" for the Temple to the large Jewish community who remained in Babylon from the time of the Prophet until they were forced to leave in 1948. Actually only 42,000 Jews left Babylon to return to Jerusalem in the time of Ezra and Nehemiah.

Ezekiel 2:9-3:3

> The eating of the Scroll implies a complete merging of the man and his message.

Ezek. 3:12
Then the spirit took me up, and I heard behind me a voice of a great rushing, *saying,* Blessed *be* the glory of the LORD from his place.

> "from" (departs out of). See Section I, Chapter 4 subhead: The departure and return of the glory.

Ezek. 3:14-17
> The Lord gave Ezekiel a mission, but God closed his mouth because the people would not receive his message. He had to remain dumb (verses 25-27) until the twelfth year of the captivity when an escapee came with the news that Jerusalem was destroyed. (Ezekiel 33:21, 22). God opened his mouth, and his message was received.

Ezekiel 3:22
<u>*Yechezkel ArtScroll Note,* page 105</u>

> In preparation for another *Merkavah* vision, the prophet is told to isolate himself once more from the people and to go to the valley....
> The use of the definite article indicates that a particular valley is meant.

Ezekiel 3:23-27

Yechezkel ArtScroll Note, pages 106,107

The obduracy of the people would not permit Yechezkel to shoulder the task of the sentinel (v.17) directly. The possibility that the Temple might really be destroyed was simply unacceptable to a people nurtured on the experience of constant Divine intervention. Finding an echo in the hearts of the exiles and drowning out the words of the prophet was the message of the false prophets who maintained the collapse of Babylon and the return to Zion was only a matter of time.

For the moment then, the medium of his communication would be his actions (Chapters 4 and 5). In horrifyingly graphic detail, more eloquent than words, Yechezkel...would live through, symbolically, the terrors of the destruction and exile. Perhaps in this way a path could be found to the hearts of the people.

Oral communication would be reserved for *when I speak to you* (v. 27) i.e., formal messages from God to His people.

Yechezkel's 'dumbness,' the prohibition against speaking directly to his people as a reprove (v.26), would be lifted only when the catastrophe of undeniable historical experience would have opened the hearts of the people to his words (24:26, 27 and 33:21,22).

<u>*Notes on Ezekiel* 2006 Edition, Dr. Thomas L. Constable, Published by Sonic Light: www.soniclight.com</u>

The first part of Ezekiel's ministry consisted of predicting the fall of Jerusalem from Babylon (chs. 1—24). When it fell in 586 B.C., he then began predicting God's judgment on the Gentile nations (chs. 25—32) and the restoration of Israel (chs. 33—48).

SECTION II

Commentary on The Book of Ezekiel

Ezekiel Chapters 4 and 5

Chapter 4

• God commands Yechezkel to act out the forthcoming siege of Jerusalem.

• A year for a day symbolizing the years of their sin.

> 390 Days of immobility for the Family of Israel (v. 5).
>
>> The Northern Kingdom
>> Ten Tribes
>
> 40 Days of immobility for the Family of Judah
>
>> The Southern Kingdom
>> Judah and Benjamin

Chapter 5

• Ezekiel commanded to shave hair and beard and to use his hairs to show what will happen to Jerusalem's peoples individually.

Deals with the destruction of Jerusalem.
Ezekiel's audience in Babylon would experience this only vicariously.

> **Ezekiel 5:12** *Yechezkel ArtScrolls*
> One third of you shall die by the plague, and with famine will they be consumed in your midst; a third by the sword will fall around you; and a third will I scatter to every direction, and unsheathe a sword after them.

God continuously, through the prophets, warned his people and their leaders.
God previously, through Jeremiah, had warned King Zedekiah and gave him a way of escape:

> **Jer. 38:17** Then said Jeremiah unto Zedekiah, Thus saith the LORD, the God of hosts, the God of Israel; If thou wilt assuredly go forth unto the king of Babylon's princes, then thy soul shall live, and this city shall not be burned with fire; and thou shalt live, and thine house:

> **Jer. 38:18** But if thou wilt not go forth to the king of Babylon's princes, then shall this city be given into the hand of the Chaldeans, and they shall burn it with fire, and thou shalt not escape out of their hand.

Jeremiah refused and this kept Jeremiah in prison.

> **Jer. 38:28** So Jeremiah abode in the court of the prison until the day that Jerusalem was taken: and he was *there* when Jerusalem was taken.

Compare with the warning given by Jesus 40 years before the destruction of Jerusalem by Titus the Roman. (Luke 21:20-24)

Josephus, Wars of the Jews [Book VI] pages 582 and 583 is printed in the Appendix for you to see God's mercy.

Consider God's revealed will for all that were carried away captive from Jerusalem unto Babylon.

> **Jer. 29:4** Thus saith the LORD of hosts, the God of Israel, unto all that are carried away captives, whom I have caused to be carried away from Jerusalem unto Babylon;
> **Jer. 29:5** Build ye houses, and dwell *in them;* and plant gardens, and eat the fruit of them;
> **Jer. 29:6** Take ye wives, and beget sons and daughters; and take wives for your sons, and give your daughters to husbands, that they may bear sons and daughters; that ye may be increased there, and not diminished.
> **Jer. 29:7** And seek the peace of the city whither I have caused you to be carried away captives, and pray unto the LORD for it: for in the peace thereof shall ye have peace.

SECTION II

Commentary on The Book of Ezekiel

Ezekiel Chapters 6 and 7

Judgments of Israel for Idolatry

Ezekiel Chapter 6

I. Prophecy reflecting judgment against the Mountains of Israel

> **Ezek. 6:1** And the word of the LORD came unto me, saying,
> **Ezek. 6:2** Son of man, set thy face toward the mountains of Israel, and prophesy against them,
> **Ezek. 6:3** And say, Ye mountains of Israel, hear the word of the Lord GOD; Thus saith the Lord GOD to the mountains, and to the hills, to the rivers, and to the valleys; Behold, I, *even* I, will bring a sword upon you, and I will destroy your high places.
> **Ezek. 6:4** And your altars shall be desolate, and your images shall be broken: and I will cast down your slain *men* before your idols

II. Prophecy For Restoration of the Mountains of Israel in the Final Ingathering

> **Ezek. 36:1** Also, thou son of man, prophesy unto the mountains of Israel, and say, Ye mountains of Israel, hear the word of the LORD:...
>
> **Ezek. 36:7** Therefore thus saith the Lord GOD; I have lifted up mine hand, Surely the heathen that *are* about you, they shall bear their shame.
> **Ezek. 36:8** But ye, O mountains of Israel, ye shall shoot forth your branches, and yield your fruit to my people of Israel; for they are at hand to come.
> **Ezek. 36:9** For, behold, I *am* for you, and I will turn unto you, and ye shall be tilled and sown:
> **Ezek. 36:10** And I will multiply men upon you, all the house of Israel, *even* all of it: and the cities shall be inhabited, and the wastes shall be builded:
> **Ezek. 36:11** And I will multiply upon you man and beast; and they shall increase and bring fruit: and I will settle you after your old estates, and will do better *unto you* than at your beginnings: and ye shall know that I *am* the LORD.
> **Ezek. 36:12** Yea, I will cause men to walk upon you, *even* my people Israel; and they shall possess thee, and thou shalt be their inheritance, and thou shalt no more henceforth bereave them *of men*.

A. This "shooting forth" is the sign Jesus said to watch for to know when He will return to set up His earthly visible kingdom.

> **Luke 21:29** And he spake to them a parable; Behold the fig tree, and all the trees;
> **Luke 21:30** When they now shoot forth, ye see and know of your own selves that summer is now nigh at hand.
> **Luke 21:31** So likewise ye, when ye see these things come to pass, know ye that the kingdom of God is nigh at hand.
> **Luke 21:32** Verily I say unto you, This generation shall not pass away, till all be fulfilled.

Ezekiel Chapter 7

Further details of the judgment and destruction.

Ending with an often used phrase in this book:
==And they shall know that I AM the LORD.==

> **Ezek. 7:27** The king shall mourn, and the prince shall be clothed with desolation, and the hands of the people of the land shall be troubled: I will do unto them after their way, and according to their deserts will I judge them; and they shall know that I *am* the LORD.

God is a God of purpose, and everything He does is for His purposes and for ultimate good, even judgments.

After the Babylonian judgment, Israel the nation, never again went after idols.

> **Is. 1:27** Zion shall be redeemed with judgment, and her converts with righteousness.

> **Is. 26:9** With my soul have I desired thee in the night; yea, with my spirit within me will I seek thee early: for ==when thy judgments *are* in the earth, the inhabitants of the world will learn righteousness.==

SECTION II

Commentary on The Book of Ezekiel

Ezekiel Chapters 8, 9, 10, 11

Chapter 8

Ezek. 8:1 And it came to pass in the sixth year, in the sixth *month,* in the fifth *day* of the month, *as* I sat in mine house, and the elders of Judah sat before me, that the hand of the Lord GOD fell there upon me.
Ezek. 8:2 Then I beheld, and lo a likeness as the appearance of fire: from the appearance of his loins even downward, fire; and from his loins even upward, as the appearance of brightness, as the colour of amber.
Ezek. 8:3 And he put forth the form of an hand, and took me by a lock of mine head; and the spirit lifted me up between the earth and the heaven, and brought me in the visions of God to Jerusalem, to the door of the inner gate that looketh toward the north; where *was* the seat of the image of jealousy, which provoketh to jealousy.
Ezek. 8:4 And, behold, the glory of the God of Israel *was* there, according to the vision that I saw in the plain.

> *Yechezkel* ArtScrolls (page 152)
>
> In a prophetic vision, Yechezkel is transported to Jerusalem.
> For six more years, the doomed city would struggle on under the illusion of its indestructibility. But, unbeknown to its inhabitants, the preparations for the end were already under way.
>
> Even within the confines of the Bait HaMikdash (The Temple), the cankerous lust for idol worship was eroding the last vestiges of holiness.
> ...stage by stage the *Shechinah* was withdrawing from Its resting place...
>
> *Yechezkel* ArtScrolls
> " Once again the prophet is shown the ineffable Glory of God in a *Merkavah* vision...."

Chapter 9

Ezek. 9:3 And ==the glory of the God of Israel was gone up from the cherub,== whereupon he was, to the threshold of the house. And he called to the man clothed with linen, which *had* the writer's inkhorn by his side;

Ezek. 9:4 And the LORD said unto him, Go through the midst of the city, through the midst of Jerusalem, and set a mark upon the foreheads of the men that sigh and that cry for all the abominations that be done in the midst thereof.

==Beginning of the withdrawal of the *Shechinah;*==

God orders Heavenly beings to mark the foreheads of those loyal to Him.
And to carry out judgment on those who committed the abominations.

Yechezkel ArtScrolls Note, Page 172
Then the Glory of the God Israel rose up from the Cheruv.
From upon the lid [of the ark] where the *Shechinah* had rested up to now, it began a gradual ten-stage withdrawal from the Temple. This is the first stage [of withdrawal]: from the Cheruv to the threshold of the Holy of Holies (Rashi).

The Talmud (Rosh Hashanah 31a) details the ten stages of withdrawal.

Brim Note:
See Exodus 25:10-22 for the description of the Ark, the Mercy Seat, and the Cherubim. It was the place of the *Shechinah* Presence of God as He dwelt among His people, first in the Tabernacle and then in the Temple. It was the place where God would communicate with His people.

> **Ex. 25:22** And there I will meet with thee, and I will commune with thee from above the mercy seat, from between the two cherubims which *are* upon the ark of the testimony, of all *things* which I will give thee in commandment unto the children of Israel.

Ezekiel 9:4-11

Men are marked in their foreheads to be saved, or to be destroyed.
Judgment begins at the house of the Lord.
God will mark the 144,000 in their foreheads. (Revelation 14:1.)
Satanic mark of the beast is in the foreheads and right hands.
(Revelation 13:16, 17.)

Brim Note: Re The Ezekiel Tablets. The 12th tablet, black basalt, begins with Ezekiel 9:7 and ends with 10:9.
The Tablets are of different materials. Light marble, etc. However some are of black basalt. Perhaps black was chosen because the abominations are written upon them. This is my own opinion.

Chapter 10

Ezek. 10:1 Then I looked, and, behold, in the firmament that was above the head of the cherubims there appeared over them as it were a sapphire stone, as the appearance of the likeness of a throne.
Ezek. 10:2 And he spake unto the man clothed with linen, and said, Go in between the wheels, *even* under the cherub, and fill thine hand with coals of fire from between the cherubims, and scatter *them* over the city. And he went in in my sight.
Ezek. 10:3 Now the cherubims stood on the right side of the house, when the man went in; and the cloud filled the inner court.
Ezek. 10:4 Then the glory of the LORD went up from the cherub, *and stood* over the threshold of the house; and the house was filled with the cloud, and the court was full of the brightness of the LORD'S glory.

Ezek. 10:18 Then the glory of the LORD departed from off the threshold of the house, and stood over the cherubims.
Ezek. 10:19 And the cherubims lifted up their wings, and mounted up from the earth in my sight: when they went out, the wheels also *were* beside them, and *every one* stood at the door of the east gate of the LORD'S house; and the glory of the God of Israel *was* over them above.

> Continued withdrawal of the *Shechinah.*

> The Chariot (*Merkavah*) accompanies, or even transports, the *Shechinah.*

Chapter 11

> The fate of the city's inhabitants is sealed

> The future lies with the exiles.

Ezek. 11:13 And it came to pass, when I prophesied, that Pelatiah the son of Benaiah died. Then fell I down upon my face, and cried with a loud voice, and said, Ah Lord GOD! wilt thou make a full end of the remnant of Israel?

> When the prophet is required to pronounce, Palatiah falls dead and Ezekiel cries out to God.

> The Lord answers with the promise of the Ingathering of "all the house of Israel" (v. 15) from out of "the countries" where they have been scattered.

> The encouraging prophecy looks past the then present Babylonian scattering, through all the days of the Jewish diaspora, to the future Ingathering at the end of days which will include all the House of Israel (The northern kingdom, the ten tribes—as well as the southern kingdom, the House of Judah). God tells the end from the beginning.

Even in the very midst of the declaration of judgment and destruction, the LORD gives them a Word of the Ingathering and of Restoration and Redemption. And notice, He calls them My people.

Ezek. 11:16 Therefore say, Thus saith the Lord GOD; Although I have cast them far off among the heathen, and although I have scattered them among the countries, yet will I be to them as a little sanctuary in the countries where they shall come.
Ezek. 11:17 Therefore say, Thus saith the Lord GOD; I will even gather you from the people, and assemble you out of the countries where ye have been scattered, and I will give you the land of Israel.
Ezek. 11:18 And they shall come thither, and they shall take away all the detestable things thereof and all the abominations thereof from thence.
Ezek. 11:19 And I will give them one heart, and I will put a new spirit within you; and I will take the stony heart out of their flesh, and will give them an heart of flesh:
Ezek. 11:20 That they may walk in my statutes, and keep mine ordinances, and do them: and they shall be my people, and I will be their God.
Ezek. 11:21 But *as for them* whose heart walketh after the heart of their detestable things and their abominations, I will recompense their way upon their own heads, saith the Lord GOD.

The Shechinah completes its withdrawal from Jerusalem.

Ezek. 11:22 Then did the cherubims lift up their wings, and the wheels beside them; and **the glory of the God of Israel *was* over them above.**
Ezek. 11:23 **And the glory of the LORD went up from the midst of the city, and stood upon the mountain which *is* on the east side of the city.**

The mountain on the east side of the city is The Mount of Olives.
Consider that the Lord ascended into Heaven from The Mount of Olives.

And when He returns to the earth, His feet shall stand on The Mount of Olives. (Acts 1:2.)

> **Zech. 14:3** Then shall the LORD go forth, and fight against those nations, as when he fought in the day of battle.
> **Zech. 14:4** And his feet shall stand in that day upon the mount of Olives, which *is* before Jerusalem on the east, and the mount of Olives shall cleave in the midst thereof toward the east and toward the west, *and there shall be* a very great valley; and half of the mountain shall remove toward the north, and half of it toward the south.

Ezek. 11:24 Afterwards the spirit took me up, and brought me in a vision by the Spirit of God into Chaldea, to them of the captivity. So the vision that I had seen went up from me.
Ezek. 11:25 Then I spake unto them of the captivity all the things that the LORD had shewed me.

> The Spirit of God transports the Prophet back to Babylon and the captivity there.

Fast Forward to the Future and Chapters 40, 43, 44, and 48
The Glory Returns

Ezek. 40:1 In the five and twentieth year of our captivity, in the beginning of the year, in the tenth *day* of the month, in the fourteenth year after that the city was smitten, in the selfsame day the hand of the LORD was upon me, and brought me thither.
Ezek. 40:2 In the visions of God brought He me into the land of Israel, and set me upon a very high mountain, by which *was* as the frame of a city on the south.

> This vision happened twenty years after Yechezkel's first prophecy.
>
> The prophecy is of earthly Jerusalem rebuilt.
>
> > *ArtScrolls*
> > Near the Temple Mount upon which Yechezkel was placed in his vision was the rebuilt city of Jerusalem (*Radak*).
>
> The Millennial Temple—probably built by the King Messiah

The Glory Returns, Never to depart.

> *ArtScrolls*
> "A very high mountain"
> In Messianic times the Temple Mount will be very high (*Rashi*, based on Isaiah 2:2).

Ezek. 43:1 Afterward he brought me to the gate, *even* the gate that looketh toward the east:
Ezek. 43:2 And, behold, the glory of the God of Israel came from the way of the east: and his voice *was* like a noise of many waters: and the earth shined with his glory.
Ezek. 43:3 And *it was* according to the appearance of the vision which I saw, *even* according to the vision that I saw when I came to destroy the city: and the visions *were* like the vision that I saw by the river Chebar; and I fell upon my face.
Ezek. 43:4 And the glory of the LORD came into the house by the way of the gate whose prospect *is* toward the east.
Ezek. 43:5 So the spirit took me up, and brought me into the inner court; and, behold, the glory of the LORD filled the house.
Ezek. 43:6 And I heard *him* speaking unto me out of the house; and the man stood by me.
Ezek. 43:7 And he said unto me, Son of man, the place of my throne, and the place of the soles of my feet, where I will dwell in the midst of the children of Israel for ever, and my holy name, shall the house of Israel no more defile, *neither* they, nor their kings, by their whoredom, nor by the carcases of their kings in their high places.

Ezekiel 40:4
...Relate all that you see to the family of Israel.

Yezkiel ArtScrolls

Ezekiel is exhorted to pass his vision on to the people. It is necessary that they be made aware of God's undying love for them, in order that they be stimulated to a true repentance. This idea is amplified at 43:10,11.

Yezkiel ArtScrolls
Yezkiel 40:3, 5
3 Now He brought me there and behold! A man whose appearance was like that of copper with a linen cord in his hand and a measuring rod, as he stood by the gate...5 And behold! There was a wall outside the House, surrounding it. And in the man's hand was a measuring rod of six cubits—each of a cubit and a handbreadth—and he measured the width of the building...and the height....

Yezkiel ArtScrolls
"Outside the house and surrounding it"
Chapter 45 (vs 1-4) describes a piece of land which is to be set aside as a gift sacred to God to the north of the city. In its exact center lies a piece of land, measuring 500 rods by 500 rods, that is to be called the Har HaBayt, Temple Mount. At six cubits to the rod, this gives us an area of 9,000,000 square cubits. By contrast the Temple Mount of the Second Temple was only 250,000 square cubits, as recorded in *Middos* 2:1.

Yechezkel ArtScrolls
Chapter 43, 44
Yechezkel is brought back to the eastern gate to witness the high drama of the Shechinah's return...

Yechezkel 43:1-7
Then he led me to the gate, the gate which opens the east. 2 And behold!—the Glory of the God of Israel came from the east, with a sound like the sound of great waters, and the earth shone with His Glory. 3 And the vision was like [the] vision that I had seen: like the vision that I had seen when I came to destroy the city, and visions like the vision that I had seen at the River Kevar. Then I fell upon my face. 4 The Glory of HASHEM entered the House through the gate which opened to the east. 5 Then a wind lifted me up and brought me into the inner courtyard; and behold!—the Glory of HASHEM filled the House.

    6 I heard Him addressing Himself to me from the House. A man was standing near me. 7 And He said to me: Ben Adam! This is the site of My throne, this is the site of My footstool where I will dwell amid the children of Israel forever....

***Yechezkel Artscrolls* 44:1-4**
Then he brought me back toward the outer gate of the Sanctuary which faces eastward, and it was closed. 2 Then HASHEM said to me: This gate shall remain closed, not to be opened, that no man may enter by it. Because HASHEM, God of Israel entered by it, it shall remain closed 3 for the prince. He is a prince—He shall sit within it to eat food before HASHEM. Through the hall of the gate He is to come, and depart that way. Then He brought me in the direction of the northern gate to the front of the House and I beheld, and see! ==The Glory of HASHEM filled the house of HASHEM.== So I fell upon my face.

For now we move forward to the glorious words which end the Book of the Prophet Ezekiel:

Ezek. 48:35 KJV
It was round about eighteen thousand *measures:* and the name of the city from *that* day *shall be,* The LORD *is* there.

> <u>*Yechezkel ArtScrolls*</u>
> Ezekiel 48:35
> ...And the name of the city from that day—HASHEM-is-there.
>
> The Lord is There = *Jehovah Shammah*

SECTION II

Commentary on The Book of Ezekiel

Ezekiel Chapters 12 - 19

Chapters 12 – 16

Chapter 12
Prophetic Symbolic Acts

Chapter 13
Prophecy against false prophets

Chapter 14
See verses referring to great intercessors: Noah, Daniel, and Job
Verses 14 and 19

Chapter 15
Israel likened to the vine
For Israel there can be no secular existence.

Chapter 16
God's dealings with Israel as His wife.
In the early days of their relationship, how He found her.
How He adorned her.

> **Ezek. 16:6** And when I passed by thee, and saw thee polluted in thine own blood, I said unto thee *when thou wast* in thy blood, Live; yea, I said unto thee *when thou wast* in thy blood, Live.
>
> **Ezek. 16:9** Then washed I thee with water; yea, I throughly washed away thy blood from thee, and I anointed thee with oil.
> **Ezek. 16:10** I clothed thee also with broidered work, and shod thee with badgers' skin, and I girded thee about with fine linen, and I covered thee with silk.
> **Ezek. 16:11** I decked thee also with ornaments, and I put bracelets upon thy hands, and a chain on thy neck.
> **Ezek. 16:12** And I put a jewel on thy forehead, and earrings in thine ears, and a beautiful crown upon thine head.
> **Ezek. 16:13** Thus wast thou decked with gold and silver; and thy raiment *was* of fine linen, and silk, and broidered work; thou didst eat fine flour, and honey, and oil: and thou wast exceeding beautiful, and thou didst prosper into a kingdom.

Ezek. 16:14 And thy renown went forth among the heathen [*goyim*, nations] for thy beauty: for it *was* perfect through my comeliness, which I had put upon thee, saith the Lord GOD.

Israel was unfaithful.

Ezek. 16:15 But thou didst trust in thine own beauty, and playedst the harlot because of thy renown, and pouredst out thy fornications on every one that passed by; his it was.

After all that goes above, God repeats and confirms His everlasting covenant relationship with Israel.

Ezek. 16:60 Nevertheless I will remember my covenant with thee in the days of thy youth, and I will establish unto thee an everlasting covenant.
Ezek. 16:61 Then thou shalt remember thy ways, and be ashamed, when thou shalt receive thy sisters, thine elder and thy younger: and I will give them unto thee for daughters, but not by thy covenant.
Ezek. 16:62 And I will establish my covenant with thee; and thou shalt know that I *am* the LORD:
Ezek. 16:63 That thou mayest remember, and be confounded, and never open thy mouth any more because of thy shame, when I am pacified toward thee for all that thou hast done, saith the Lord GOD.

Jeremiah too was a prophet to Israel before and during the Babylonian captivity. The sages say that everything God does for Israel is based upon the faith she portrayed when she followed Him into an "unsown" wilderness. (Jeremiah 2:2.) Thus indicating her complete faith in Him. And the very opposite of Ezekiel 16:15 and the verses that follow it, in which she trusted in her "own beauty" and others, rather than completely trusting Him. Consider what the Lord said through Jeremiah.

Jer. 2:1 Moreover the word of the LORD came to me, saying,
Jer. 2:2 Go and cry in the ears of Jerusalem, saying, Thus saith the LORD; I remember thee, the kindness of thy youth, the love of thine espousals, when thou wentest after me in the wilderness, in a land *that was* not sown.
Jer. 2:3 Israel *was* holiness unto the LORD, *and* the firstfruits of his increase: all that devour him shall offend; evil shall come upon them, saith the LORD.

Chapters 17 – 19
Short Summaries from
Through the Bible Book by Book
by Myer Perleman
Gospel Publishing House, Springfield, MO

Chapter 17
In the parable of the great eagle is shown the punishment of Zedekiah's treachery in breaking his covenant with Nebuchadnezzar, and in calling the aid of Egypt in rebelling against him.

Chapter 18
Jehovah's vindication of Himself against the charge that He was punishing the present generation for the sins of their fathers.

Chapter 19
A lamentation over the fall of the house of David.

SECTION II

Commentary on The Book of Ezekiel

Ezekiel Chapter 20

God's Plan to Reveal and Sanctify His Name to the Nations Through Israel

Ezek. 20:5 And say unto them, Thus saith the Lord GOD; In the day when I chose Israel, and lifted up mine hand unto the seed of the house of Jacob, and made myself known unto them in the land of Egypt, when I lifted up mine hand unto them, saying, I *am* the LORD your God;
Ezek. 20:6 In the day *that* I lifted up mine hand unto them, to bring them forth of the land of Egypt into a land that I had espied for them, flowing with milk and honey, which *is* the glory of all lands:
Ezek. 20:7 Then said I unto them, Cast ye away every man the abominations of his eyes, and defile not yourselves with the idols of Egypt: I *am* the LORD your God.
Ezek. 20:8 But they rebelled against me, and would not hearken unto me: they did not every man cast away the abominations of their eyes, neither did they forsake the idols of Egypt: then I said, I will pour out my fury upon them, to accomplish my anger against them in the midst of the land of Egypt.
Ezek. 20:9 But I wrought for my name's sake, that it should not be polluted before the heathen, among whom they *were,* in whose sight I made myself known unto them, in bringing them forth out of the land of Egypt.

The phrase "I lifted up mine hand" indicates that God swears this.

ArtScrolls Introduction (p 314)
In this chapter God reveals to Yechezkel that the underlying factor and prime mover in the history of *Knesset Israel,* The Community of Israel, is the imperative of *the Sanctification of God's Name.*
(See comm. to v. 9 for an elaboration of this concept).

ArtScrolls Yechezkel 20:8, 9
And I intended to pour My fury upon them, to spend My anger on them, in the midst of the land of Egypt. 9 But I acted for the sake of My Name, that it not be desecrated in the eyes of the nations midst which they are; in whose sight I had made Myself known to them to remove them from the land of Egypt.

ArtScrolls
The idea that Israel is permitted to survive in order to avoid Desecration of the Name does not start with Yechezkel. Numbers 14:13-20 teaches that it was just such an argument offered by Moses, which caused God to forgive the people for the sin of the spies; and Deut 32:26 teaches the same concept.

Ezek. 20:33 *As* I live, saith the Lord GOD, surely with a mighty hand, and with a stretched out arm, and with fury poured out, will I rule over you:
Ezek. 20:34 And I will bring you out from the people, and will gather you out of the countries wherein ye are scattered, with a mighty hand, and with a stretched out arm, and with fury poured out.
Ezek. 20:35 And I will bring you into the wilderness of the people, and there will I plead with you face to face.
Ezek. 20:36 Like as I pleaded with your fathers in the wilderness of the land of Egypt, so will I plead with you, saith the Lord GOD.
Ezek. 20:37 And I will cause you to pass under the rod, and I will bring you into the bond of the covenant:
Ezek. 20:38 And I will purge out from among you the rebels, and them that transgress against me: I will bring them forth out of the country where they sojourn, and they shall not enter into the land of Israel: and ye shall know that I *am* the LORD.
Ezek. 20:39 As for you, O house of Israel, thus saith the Lord GOD; Go ye, serve ye every one his idols, and hereafter *also,* if ye will not hearken unto me: but pollute ye my holy name no more with your gifts, and with your idols.
Ezek. 20:40 For in mine holy mountain, in the mountain of the height of Israel, saith the Lord GOD, there shall all the house of Israel, all of them in the land, serve me: there will I accept them, and there will I require your offerings, and the firstfruits of your oblations, with all your holy things.
Ezek. 20:41 I will accept you with your sweet savour, when I bring you out from the people, and gather you out of the countries wherein ye have been scattered; and I will be sanctified in you before the heathen.
Ezek. 20:42 And ye shall know that I *am* the LORD, when I shall bring you into the land of Israel, into the country *for* the which I lifted up mine hand to give it to your fathers.
Ezek. 20:43 And there shall ye remember your ways, and all your doings, wherein ye have been defiled; and ye shall lothe yourselves in your own sight for all your evils that ye have committed.
Ezek. 20:44 And ye shall know that I *am* the LORD, when I have wrought with you for my name's sake, not according to your wicked ways, nor according to your corrupt doings, O ye house of Israel, saith the Lord GOD.

Brim Note:
Again, in the very midst of the prophecies of judgment and purging, God restates the assuredness of His Covenant with Israel. And of the fact that it shall include "all the House of Israel," in the Land of Israel.
We are so blessed to live in the days when He has reestablished the Nation of Israel and is gathering the Jews there.

ArtScrolls
"And I will be hallowed through you in the eyes of the nations."
[The Hebrew word used here] in Yechezkel usually means that God's Name will be hallowed through His deeds. Thus the meaning would be that God's name will be hallowed when the nations of the world see the ingathering of the exiles...

This thought pervades Yechezkel's prophecy (28:25, 26:23) and with it he concludes his teachings (39:27-29) before embarking on the vision of the... final Holy Temple.

Brim Note:
Would God that the Nations could see the very revelation of the reality of God and His Word in His doing what He said He would do, bring the scattered Jews back to the Land He promised them forever.

Those Nations who see it, and cooperate with it, will know the blessings of God now in the end of this age. And eventually in the judgment of the Nations, go into the Millennium as sheep nations. (Matthew 25.)

SECTION II

Commentary on The Book of Ezekiel

Ezekiel Chapters 21 - 23

Ezekiel 21

The Sharpened Sword
    The human sword is Nebuchadnezzar (vv 9, 10, 19).
    But the decree of judgment that allows its use is of the LORD.

The Promised King Messiah
    Again in the midst of judgment, the promise of the Messiah.
    (v 27; Genesis 49:10.)

Ezekiel 22

ArtScrolls, page 371.
The bitter denunciation of Jerusalem in this chapter is unparalleled in Scripture.... The greatest falls occur from the greatest heights.

<u>Brim Note:</u> Yet even midst the gross sin that brought on the judgment, God looked for an intercessor:

> **Ezek. 22:30** And I sought for a man among them, that should make up the hedge, and stand in the gap before me for the land, that I should not destroy it: but I found none.
> **Ezek. 22:31** Therefore have I poured out mine indignation upon them; I have consumed them with the fire of my wrath: their own way have I recompensed upon their heads, saith the Lord GOD.

Ezekiel 23

The two kingdoms are presented as two sister states.

    Aholah =   The Northern Kingdom, Samaria (Shomron)
                   Also sometimes identified as Israel.
    Aholivah =   The Southern Kingdom, identified by its
                   capital, Jerusalem.
                   Sometimes called Judah.

SECTION II

Commentary on The Book of Ezekiel

Ezekiel Chapter 24

The day had come. Yechezkel's prophecies of destruction had come to their terrible climax

Ezek. 24:1 Again in the ninth year, in the tenth month, in the tenth *day* of the month, the word of the LORD came unto me, saying,
Ezek. 24:2 Son of man [*Ben Adam*], write thee the name of the day, *even* of this same day: the king of Babylon set himself against Jerusalem this same day.

The dates of the happenings of the destruction of the First Temple became fast dates. They are remembrances of terrible things. However, the Bible says they will one day be turned into "joy and gladness" (Zechariah 8:19).

I. The fast of the 17th of Tammuz, the first of the four fast days accepted by prophetic degree. Tisha B'Av. And two others.

    A. The 17th of Tammuz

        • Moses descended from Mt Sinai. Saw the golden calf. Smashed the Tablets.

        • King Menashe set up an idol in the Temple.

        • Siege of Jerusalem by Babylon begins.

        • Romans breached Jerusalem's walls 70 AD.

    B. Tisha B'Av — 9th of Av
       Saddest day in the Year.

        • Anniversary of the Divine decree that the Jewish people remain in the desert for 40 years till that generation died out, after they cried all night over the 12 spies' evil report of the land and accepted it (Numbers 13,14).

        • First Temple destroyed by Babylonians in 586 BC.

        • Second Temple destroyed by Romans 70 AD.

- 1492, Av 9 the last day by which all Jews had to leave Spain in Spanish Inquisition.

- World War I begins on Av 9, leading to WWII and Holocaust.

- 2005 Government of Israel under Prime Minister Ariel Sharon push Jews out of Gush Katif (Gaza). (The day originally picked by Sharon government was 9 Av. When they discovered their mistake in choosing that day, they decided to wait until after the fast.)

C. Four fast dates. Now mournful. Shall be turned into joy.

<u>David Baron, *Zechariah, A Commentary*... Pages 248, 249</u>
The fast of the 9th day of the 4th month was instituted to celebrate the taking of the city by Nebuchadnezzar in the 11th year of Zedekiah's reign (Jer. 52:6,7). The fast of the 5th month (the blackest day of all the Jewish calendar) commemorates the destruction of both the city and the Temple (2 Kings 25:25, 26; Jer. 41:1-3) and many other calamities which...happened on this same day. The fast of the 7th month...was appointed for the murder of Gedaliah. The fast of the 10th commemorated the commencement of the siege of Jerusalem on the 10th day of that month in the 9th year of Zedekiah.

All these days are still observed as fasts by the Jewish nation in all parts of the earth...
==But the long night of weeping is to be followed by a morning of joy, when Jehovah shall accomplish the "good" which He has purposed and promised to Israel and Jerusalem (Zechariah 8:14, 15), and then the former troubles and calamities shall be "forgotten" (Isaiah 65:16), and the very days which commemorate them shall be turned into "joy and gladness" and *moedim tovim*, cheerful feasts.==

II. Ezekiel the Prophet living example at death of his wife. (v. 16.)

III. Verses 26, 27
Fugitive comes with the news of Jerusalem's destruction.
Prophet's mouth opened.
He takes his place. Receives their respect.
(See Appendix *Mother of the Pound* for how respect endured thru centuries.)
They recognize that a prophet has been among them.

SECTION II

Commentary on The Book of Ezekiel

Ezekiel Chapter 25

Judgments Against Neighboring Nations
Ammon, Moab, Edom, the Philistines

Dr. Billye Brim, *Judgment of the Nations for How They Treat Israel,* Pages 5, 6

The first mention of the nations (Heb. *goyim*) is in Genesis 10. After the flood, the chapter lists the sons of Noah's three sons: Shem, Ham, and Yapheth. Seventy foundational nations are listed. The Lord's will for them was, *"Be fruitful, and multiply, and replenish the earth"* (Gen. 9:1). Under Nimrod (Gen. 10:8-11), the nations rebelled at Babel (Gen. 11). Three hundred and forty years after the flood, they had not scattered but were bunched up on the plain of Shinar (Babylon). The Babylonian System began with this rebellion. The LORD judged them, confused their language, and scattered them throughout the earth.

In Genesis 12, He introduced His separated nation, Israel. Israel was separated *from* the nations and *unto* God with *the call of revealing God to the nations.* In God's revelation to the church regarding Israel in Romans Chapters 9, 10, and 11, He avers that He does not change His mind regarding this calling. *"For the gifts and the calling of God are not repented of"* (Rom. 11:29). Nations as nations, therefore are judged as to how they treat the nation with the call to reveal God to them.

> Notice that in the judgments pronounced herein, the Just God gives the cause for the judgments saying, *"Because....."*

> **Prov. 26:2** As the bird by wandering, as the swallow by flying, so the curse **causeless** shall not come.

I. Ammon and Moab

    A. Children of Lot by his daughters

    B. Ancient territory in what is now Jordan
        (Jordan's capital is Amman.)

        Ezek. 25:2 Son of man, set thy face against the Ammonites, and prophesy against them;

> **Ezek. 25:3** And say unto the Ammonites, Hear the word of the Lord GOD; Thus saith the Lord GOD; Because thou saidst, Aha, against my sanctuary, when it was profaned; and against the land of Israel, when it was desolate; and against the house of Judah, when they went into captivity;...
>
> **Ezek. 25:6** For thus saith the Lord GOD; Because thou hast clapped *thine* hands, and stamped with the feet, and rejoiced in heart with all thy despite against the land of Israel;
> **Ezek. 25:7** Behold, therefore I will stretch out mine hand upon thee, land of Israel, when it was desolate; and against the house of Judah, when they went into captivity;

II. Edom

    A.   Children of Esau.

    B.   Ancient territory just south of Ammon and Moab.

    C.   A rather widely accepted idea among religious Jews is that Edom equates with Rome. I do not see this. But it could be.

> **Ezek. 25:12** Thus saith the Lord GOD; Because that Edom hath dealt against the house of Judah by taking vengeance, and hath greatly offended, and revenged himself upon them;
> **Ezek. 25:13** Therefore thus saith the Lord GOD; I will also stretch out mine hand upon Edom,...

III. Philistines

    A.   Foreign peoples who came by way of the Sea and settled in what is now known as Gaza.

> **Ezek. 25:15** Thus saith the Lord GOD; Because the Philistines have dealt by revenge, and have taken vengeance with a despiteful heart, to destroy *it* for the old hatred;
> **Ezek. 25:16** Therefore thus saith the Lord GOD; Behold, I will stretch out mine hand upon the Philistines,...

SECTION II

Commentary on The Book of Ezekiel

Ezekiel Chapters 26, 27, 28

The Judgment of Tyre

Tyre was a proud city-state who considered her rocky island fortress, impregnable. But God pronounces judgment upon her, and history confirms that it happened just as God said it would. (See Appendix: *The Destruction of Tyre.*)

Zidon is associated with Tyre in Scripture.

Again, the LORD uses "because."

> **Ezek. 26:2** Son of man, because that Tyrus hath said against Jerusalem, Aha, she is broken *that was* the gates of the people: she is turned unto me: I shall be replenished, *now* she is laid waste:
> **Ezek. 26:3** Therefore thus saith the Lord GOD; Behold, I *am* against thee, O Tyrus, and will cause many nations to come up against thee, as the sea causeth his waves to come up.
> **Ezek. 26:4** And they shall destroy the walls of Tyrus, and break down her towers: I will also scrape her dust from her, and make her like the top of a rock.
> **Ezek. 26:5** It shall be *a place for* the spreading of nets in the midst of the sea: for I have spoken *it*, saith the Lord GOD: and it shall become a spoil to the nations.

So gross is her arrogance, three chapters are devoted to her judgment. However, insight into Satan and his influence on nations is given in Chapter 28.

Chapter 28
A Double Kingdom System

<u>The Prince of Tyre</u>

> The prideful earthly ruler of Tyre.

> In the following verse, God addresses one he calls "The Prince of Tyre."
> He lifts himself up as a god, but God says, he is only a man. The Prince of Tyre here is the earthly ruler of Tyre.

> **Ezek. 28:2** Son of man, say unto the prince of Tyrus, Thus saith the Lord GOD; Because thine heart *is* lifted up, and thou hast said, I *am* a God, I sit *in* the seat of God, in the midst of the seas; yet thou *art* a man, and not God, though thou set thine heart as the heart of God:

The King of Tyre

A ruler over Tyre from the mid-heavens – he is not a man, but a spirit being.

A prince of the powers of the air who rules down through the earthly ruler (Ephesians 2:2).

His description reveals that he is Lucifer turned Satan.

He has been in Eden (v. 13).

He is a created being, not born as men (vv. 13, 15).

He was the anointed cherub upon the heaven holy mountain of God (v.14).

He walked up and down in the midst of the stones of fire (v. 14).

He was perfect in the day he was created until iniquity was found in him (v. 15).

> *Where did the iniquity come from?*
> God created an archangel. Lucifer made a devil out of himself. Lifted up in pride, he was the first ever to turn his God-given free will against God.
>
> *Isaiah 14 answers the question.*
> Translators put in the punctuation. The original Hebrew has no punctuation. Question marks should have been used in verse 12 rather than exclamation marks.
>
> Notice his five rebellious "I wills."
>
>> **Is. 14:12** How art thou fallen from heaven, O Lucifer, son of the morning! *how* art thou cut down to the ground, which didst weaken the nations!
>> **Is. 14:13** For thou hast said in thine heart, I will ascend into heaven, I will exalt my throne above the stars of God: I will sit also upon the mount of the congregation, in the sides of the north:
>> **Is. 14:14** I will ascend above the heights of the clouds; I will be like the most High.
>> **Is. 14:15** Yet thou shalt be brought down to hell, to the sides of the pit.

Isaiah 14 also reveals his evil influence on nations, as does Revelation 20:7 and 8.

Future Ingathering
Associated With End of Days Judgment Upon Israel's Neighboring Nations

Ezek. 28:24 And there shall be no more a pricking brier unto the house of Israel, nor *any* grieving thorn of all *that are* round about them, that despised them; and they shall know that I *am* the Lord GOD.
Ezek. 28:25 Thus saith the Lord GOD; When I shall have gathered the house of Israel from the people among whom they are scattered, and shall be sanctified in them in the sight of the heathen [*goyim,* nations], then shall they dwell in their land that I have given to my servant Jacob.
Ezek. 28:26 And they shall dwell safely therein, and shall build houses, and plant vineyards; yea, they shall dwell with confidence, when I have executed judgments upon all those that despise them round about them; and they shall know that I *am* the LORD their God.

Again, the Lord gives the promise of future blessing.
God tells the end from the beginning.

"they shall know that I am the Lord God."
"they shall know that I am the LORD their God."
This phrase is often used in this Book.
It shows God's purpose in the various blessings, or judgments.

"my servant Jacob"
When God speaks about the physical descendants of Abraham, He often calls them "Jacob." He doesn't call them "Abraham." Abraham had several other sons. He doesn't call them "Isaac." Isaac had another son, Esau. He calls them "Jacob," for all Jacob's sons were the twelve tribes of Israel.

SECTION II

Commentary on The Book of Ezekiel

Ezekiel Chapters 29 - 33

Judgments of Various Nations

Chapter 29

    Judgment of Pharoah, and of Egypt

        Egypt was a superpower to the south.
        Babylon was a superpower to the north.

> **Ezek. 29:19** Therefore thus saith the Lord GOD; Behold, I will give the land of Egypt unto Nebuchadrezzar king of Babylon; and he shall take her multitude, and take her spoil, and take her prey; and it shall be the wages for his army.

Chapter 30

    Judgment of Egypt and her allies, "all that uphold Egypt" (v. 6).

Chapter 31

    Judgment of Pharoah and "all his multitude" (v. 18).

Chapter 32

    Judgment of Pharoah, Egypt.
    And other nations.
    Asshur, Elam, Meshech, Tubal, Edom, Zidon.

Chapter 33

    The Prophet is appointed a watchman unto the house of Israel (v. 7).

    The runner arrives with news of Jerusalem's destruction,
    and the prophet's mouth is opened. (vv. 21, 22.)

SECTION II

Commentary on The Book of Ezekiel

Ezekiel Chapter 34

Verses 1-10

God lays the blame squarely with the shepherds (the priests, the teachers) of Israel.

> **Ezek. 22:26** Her priests have violated my law, and have **profaned** mine **holy** things: they have put no difference between the **holy** and **profane,** neither have they shewed *difference* between the unclean and the clean...

> **Is. 5:20** Woe unto them that call **evil good,** and **good evil;** that put darkness for light, and light for darkness; that put bitter for sweet, and sweet for bitter!

Verses 11-31

Israel is God's flock.
He will save them.
He will set up One Shepherd over them.
The Ingathering of the Scattered Sheep.
The Restoration of Israel.
The Redemption of Israel.

> **Ezek. 34:11** For thus saith the Lord GOD; Behold, I, *even* I, will both search my sheep, and seek them out.
> **Ezek. 34:12** As a shepherd seeketh out his flock in the day that he is among his sheep *that are* scattered; so will I seek out my sheep, and will deliver them out of all places where they have been scattered in the cloudy and dark day.
> **Ezek. 34:13** And I will bring them out from the people, and gather them from the countries, and will bring them to their own land, and feed them upon the mountains of Israel by the rivers, and in all the inhabited places of the country.
> **Ezek. 34:14** I will feed them in a good pasture, and upon the high mountains of Israel shall their fold be: there shall they lie in a good fold, and *in* a fat pasture shall they feed upon the mountains of Israel...

Ezek. 34:23 And I will set up one shepherd over them, and he shall feed them, *even* my servant David; he shall feed them, and he shall be their shepherd.
Ezek. 34:24 And I the LORD will be their God, and my servant David a prince among them; I the LORD have spoken *it*.
Ezek. 34:25 And I will make with them a covenant of peace...

Ezek. 34:27 And the tree of the field shall yield her fruit, and the earth shall yield her increase, and they shall be safe in their land, and shall know that I *am* the LORD, when I have broken the bands of their yoke, and delivered them out of the hand of those that served themselves of them.
Ezek. 34:28 And they shall no more be a prey to the heathen [*goyim,* nations]...

Ezek. 34:30 Thus shall they know that I the LORD their God *am* with them, and *that* they, *even* the house of Israel, *are* My people, saith the Lord GOD.
Ezek. 34:31 And ye My flock, the flock of My pasture, *are* men, *and* I *am* your God, saith the Lord GOD.

So much for replacement theology!

SECTION II
Commentary on The Book of Ezekiel

Ezekiel Chapter 35

Mount Seir

Now we come to the chapters of the *then-and-now prophetic future*.....

> There are two mountain ranges separated by the Jordan rift valley:
> > The Mountains of Israel which form a vertical spine running up and down present-day Israel.
> > The Mount Seir range. The Mountains of Moab and Edom. In present-day Jordan.
>
> Ezekiel 35 is a prophesy *against* mount Seir.
> Ezekiel 36 is a prophesy *for* the Mountains of Israel.

Ezek. 35:2 Son of man, set thy face against mount Seir, and prophesy against it,
Ezek. 35:3 And say unto it, Thus saith the Lord GOD; Behold, O mount Seir, I *am* against thee, and I will stretch out mine hand against thee, and I will make thee most desolate.
Ezek. 35:4 I will lay thy cities waste, and thou shalt be desolate, and thou shalt know that I *am* the LORD.
Ezek. 35:5 Because thou hast had a perpetual hatred, and hast shed *the blood of* the children of Israel by the force of the sword in the time of their calamity, in the time *that their* iniquity *had* an end:

> Norma Archbold, *The Mountains of Israel: The Bible and the West Bank,* page 45

Mount Seir was the homeland of Esau (also called Edom) father of the Edomites.

"So Esau dwelt in Mount Seir. Esau is Edom" (Genesis 36:8).

Notice that the Lord speaks to an area called Edom or Mount Seir. This is the area where the ancient Edomites lived. Arabic people—descendants of ancient Middle East tribes such as Edom—still live there today.

Today people living in the area once known as Edom are called Arabs, Jordanians and/or Palestinians.

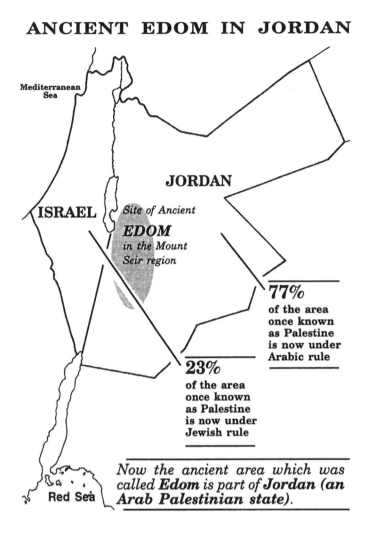

ANCICENT EDOM IN JORDAN

*Now the ancient area which was called **Edom** is part of **Jordan** (an Arab Palestinian state).*

Where was Edom?
After WWI, the land known long ago as Edom was part of the area called Palestine.

Was Palestine a state?
No, never.

Then what was Palestine?
After WWI, the British occupied land in the Middle East. Palestine was the popular name of one area in their control.

According to most reliable sources, Palestine is an English name derived from the Roman name Palaestina. When the Romans captured Judea in the first century, they called it Syria Palaestina—some believe to erase any Jewish connection to the land and to insult the Jews by using a name derived from the Philistines, Israel's ancient enemies during the time of King Saul and King David.

Who are the Palestinians?
Until 1948 residents in the area [all of the British mandate including present-day Israel and Jordan] were called 'Palestinians' and were NOT a separate race. All residents of the area (*Jews, Gentiles and Arabs*) were Palestinians. However, at that time Arabic people preferred not to be called Palestinian.

Today most people who identify themselves as Palestinians are Arabic. However, even today not all Arab residents of Israel...wish to be called Palestinians.

The former British-occupied area called Palestine is now two states—Jordan 77% (ruled by Arabs); and Israel 23% under Jewish rule. (See map.) The area, that was known as Edom in ancient times, is now part of Jordan.

Ezek. 35:5 Because thou hast had a perpetual hatred, and hast shed *the blood of* the children of Israel by the force of the sword in the time of their calamity, in the time *that their* iniquity *had* an end:

Yechezkel, ArtScrolls, Ezekiel 35:5
Because you have eternal hatred...

Ezek. 35:10 Because thou hast said, These two nations and these two countries shall be mine, and we will possess it; whereas the LORD was there:
Ezek. 35:11 Therefore, *as* I live, saith the Lord GOD, I will even do according to thine anger, and according to thine envy which thou hast used out of thy hatred against them; and I will make myself known among them, when I have judged thee.
Ezek. 35:12 And thou shalt know that I *am* the LORD, *and that* I have heard all thy blasphemies which thou hast spoken against the mountains of Israel, saying, They are laid desolate, they are given us to consume.
Ezek. 35:13 Thus with your mouth ye have boasted against me, and have multiplied your words against me: I have heard *them.*

> Brim Note:
> I believe this has to do with the present day situation.
> A so-called "a two-state solution."
> And then to "possess" the mountains of Israel.
>
> The Balfour Resolution, and the subsequent British Mandate (ratified by The League of Nations) called for Britain to watch over the territory until the Jews were able to be established a Jewish entity in their ancient homeland. It included all of present day Israel (including what the world calls The West Bank) and Jordan.
>
> Because of Arab pressure, two-thirds was divided off the mandated territory and England created Jordan. England reached outside the local populous and established a Hashemite royalty. Unrest through the years has been fermented by rebellions of the populous against the Hashemite king.
> (For more information you can research Black September Civil War in Jordan and how the fleeing PLO refugees caused civil war in Lebanon.)

Ezek. 35:14 Thus saith the Lord GOD; When the whole earth rejoiceth, I will make thee desolate.

> This clearly refers to Messianic times
>
> *Yechezkel ArtScrolls*
> When I establish My kingship, the whole world will rejoice, as it is written (Psalm 97:1). God has ruled. Let the earth jubilate. (*Rashi*)

****

Brim Note: I really like the following from Norma Archbold.

> Norma Archbold, *The Mountains of Israel: The Bible & the West Bank,* pages 56, 57.
>
> Mount Seir, Edom and the nations around Israel in chapters 35 and 36 of Ezekiel and Psalm 83, refer to the leaders of Arab Islamic groups and nations who are trying to destroy Israel.

Something to keep in mind

God is always merciful. The Psalmist calls on God to punish Edom and the nations all around. But the punishment has a purpose,

"...That they may **seek Your name,** O Lord...That they may know that **You,** whose name alone is the Lord, **are the Most High** over all the earth."
(Psalm 83:16, 18)

...as we read about the sins of Edom and *the rest of the nations all around,* please understand that the Lord wants to bring Arabic people, who are deceived by Islam, to acknowledge Him as Lord. He hopes that they will seek Him.

This must be our attitude too. Please remember that most Arabic people are Moslems and do not have the Bible. Most do not understand that they are offending the Lord when they attack Israel.

Young Arabic people who are trying to live good lives are told by Islamic religious leaders that they will be in paradise if they are killed while fighting against Israel.

While we must not condemn Arabic people for their blindness, neither should we encourage them to oppose the plan of God.

Some well-meaning, but uninformed Jewish and Christian people encourage the Palestinians to claim sovereignty over the Lord's Land—to strive for a second Palestinian state. They think they are being unselfishly just. But in reality they are misleading Palestinians by encouraging them to oppose God. Believers are responsible to know the Word of God and to warn their Arabic brothers to walk in harmony with the Lord's plan.

[Archbold] Note: While the Bible teaches that Israel will possess the Holy Land, aliens are allowed to live in Israel under Israeli rule.... Today thousands of Palestinians live in peace under Israeli law. They have homes and jobs in Israel. Some even sit as representatives in the Israeli Knesset (Congress or Parliament.)

Brim Note: The Bible speaks of strangers (non-Jews) who can live in restored Israel in a state of blessing. However, they must realize that the Land is the Promised Land of the Jews. And that those who bless Israel are blessed (Genesis 12:3). And that Promised Land is not to be divided:

KJV
Joel 3:1 For, behold, in those days, and in that time, when I shall bring again the captivity of Judah and Jerusalem,
Joel 3:2 I will also gather all nations, and will bring them down into the valley of Jehoshaphat, and will plead with them there for my people and *for* my heritage Israel, whom they have scattered among the nations, and parted my land.

Amplified
Joel 3:2 I will gather all nations and will bring them down into the Valley of Jehoshaphat, and there will I deal with *and* execute judgment upon them for [their treatment of] My people and of My heritage Israel, whom they have scattered among the nations and [because] they have divided My land.

> Brim Note: Nations and politicians who vainly try to settle the so-called Palestianian issue with a two-state solution, should heed Joel 3:2.

SECTION II

Commentary on The Book of Ezekiel

Ezekiel Chapter 36

The Mountains of Israel (The Land)

<u>Yechezkel ArtScrolls Prefatory Remarks, page 547</u>
...an extension of the previous (chapter). In contrast to Seir's mountains...desolation...Israel's hills will burst forth with a profusion of God's bounty, welcoming a reborn Israel to its eternal home.
   The theme of the chapter is renewal: renewal of the people...and renewal of the land... Thus the prophet brings us face to face with one of the great mysteries of Jewish experience—the bond between land and people which has never weakened despite centuries of exile one from another.
   (In exile) Israel would leave the land,...but its conquerors would never find the land hospitable. (Leviticus 26:32).

Ezek. 36:1 Also, thou son of man, prophesy unto the mountains of Israel, and say, Ye mountains of Israel, hear the word of the LORD:

The mountains of Israel are like a spine that runs the length of Israel. A map of present-day Israel shows the topography. On the west, running north and south, is the coastal plain. In the middle, are the mountains of Israel. At their eastern edge is the Jordan rift valley.

Earlier, the prophecy was against the mountains of Israel. Yet, even then, there was the promise of a remnant. (Ezekiel 6:1-8.)
Here the glorious restoration is told.

Ezek. 36:2 Thus saith the Lord GOD; Because the enemy hath said against you, ==Aha, even the ancient high places are ours in possession:==
Ezek. 36:3 Therefore prophesy and say, Thus saith the Lord GOD; Because they have made *you* desolate, and swallowed you up on every side, that ye might be a possession unto the residue of the heathen [*goyim,* nations] and ye are taken up in the lips of talkers, and *are* an infamy of the people:

<u>Norma Parrish Archbold, *The Mountains of Israel:*</u>
<u>*The Bible & the West Bank,* page 1.</u>
The mountains of Israel are the heart of the Land promised by God to the children of Israel. They are Judea and Samaria [*Shomron*], the inheritance of the tribes of Judah, Benjamin, and Joseph [Ephraim and Manasseh].
The West Bank and the mountains of Israel are nearly identical.

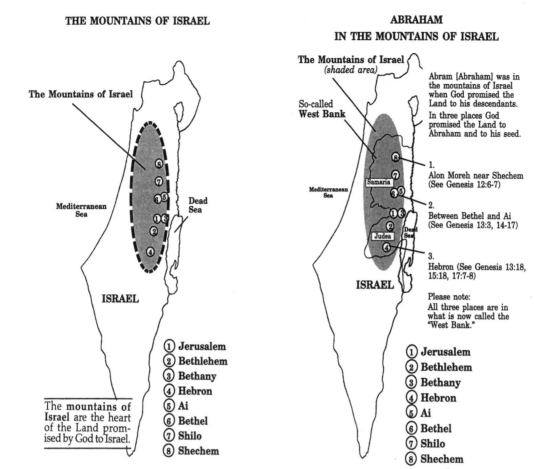

Brim Note:

"...the enemy hath said against you, Aha, even the ancient high places are ours in possession"

The Ancient high places include the places of worship. All are in the mountains, in what the world calls The West Bank.

> Shechem, Beit El, Hebron — The places of Abraham's altars.
> Shiloh — Where Joshua took the Holy Ark and it remained 369 years.
> Jerusalem, The Temple Mount — The highest place of all.

The nations, pushed upon by that one who is known as the deceiver of the nations, clamor that these holy places upon the mountains of Israel belong to others. (Revelation 20:3,8.)

See also Ezekiel 25:3. The Dome of the Rock sits atop the Temple Mount. This is an interesting verse in light of the fact that it is Jordan (whose capital is Amman), through the Islamic Waqf, that holds day-to-day management of the Temple Mount. They do not allow Jews, or any others, to pray there. Prophetic Scripture can have 'fillments', and then move on to fulfillments. I am sure Ezekiel 25:3 had earlier 'fillment' but it may also refer to today's situation. For The Temple Mount is the site of The Future Millennial Temple (Ezekiel 40-48).

Ezek. 36:3 Therefore prophesy and say, Thus saith the Lord GOD; Because they have made *you* desolate, and swallowed you up on every side, that ye might be a possession unto the residue of the heathen [*goyim*, nations], and ye are ==taken up in the lips of talkers,== and *are* an infamy of the people:

> *"taken up in the lips of talkers"*
> Nations have busied themselves with the business of the ownership of what the Bible calls Judea and Samaria [Hebrew: *Shomron*], and the world calls the West Bank.
>
> **How did it get to be called The West Bank?**
> The modern state of Israel was reborn on May 14, 1948. Immediately, seven Arab armies attacked the small reborn state. When the dust settled, Israel's portion of the Promised Land, increased from what they'd been allotted by the UN Partition Plan. However, Jordan conquered this area, and King Abdullah I called it The West Bank of the Jordan River. In 1967, Jordan joined forces with Syria and Egypt to attack Israel and "drive them into the sea." In the miraculous Six-Day War, Israel took back the so-called West Bank area. Jordan held it for only 19 years.

Ezek. 36:4 Therefore, ye mountains of Israel, hear the word of the Lord GOD; Thus saith the Lord GOD to the mountains, and to the hills, to the rivers, and to the valleys, to the desolate wastes, and to ==the cities that are forsaken,== which became a prey and derision to the residue of the heathen [*goyim*, nations] that *are* round about;
Ezek. 36:5 Therefore thus saith the Lord GOD; Surely in the fire of my jealousy have I spoken against the residue of the heathen [*goyim*], and against all Idumea, ==which have appointed My land into their possession with the joy of all *their* heart,== with despiteful minds, to cast it out for a prey.
Ezek. 36:6 Prophesy therefore concerning the land of Israel, and say unto the mountains, and to the hills, to the rivers, and to the valleys, Thus saith the Lord GOD; Behold, I have spoken in my jealousy and in my fury, because ye have borne the shame of the heathen:
Ezek. 36:7 Therefore thus saith the Lord GOD; ==I have lifted up mine hand,== Surely the heathen that *are* about you, they shall bear their shame.

> *"the cities that are forsaken"*
> These are the ancient cities of Bible times which were forsaken during the exile. The prophet is to speak to them that they will be rebuilt. Bible believing Jews are doing just that. The world makes fun of them. Calls them "settlers." (Nothing really wrong with that name.) They are demonized by most of the world press. Former Sect. of State James Baker in Bush I's cabinet said, "The West Bank Settlements are the greatest threat to world peace." And he fought consistently, dragging the U.S. with him, to dismantle these cities which God has spoken through the prophets that the Jews are to return there and build.
>
>> A "settler" once told me as we walked in his olive grove, "There are three ways we are to possess the Land as the Lord told us: Walk it. Plant it. Build on it."

"appointed My land into their possession with the joy of all their heart"
Notice God calls it "My land."
I remember watching the television coverage of when Bethlehem was handed over to Arafat. They danced in the streets as they ran up the PLO flag.

> <u>CNN, Web Posting, December 23, 1995</u>
> "PLO leader Yasser Arafat arrived for Saturday's celebration by helicopter. Like an electric current, a sudden surge of excitement spread through the crowd packed in Manger Square as the helicopter circled low over the symbol of the hillside town -- the Church of the Nativity, built over the grotto where tradition says Jesus was born 2000 years ago."

"I have lifted up mine hand"
God swears, lifting up His hand so-to-speak in an oath.

Ezek. 36:8 But ye, O mountains of Israel, ==ye shall shoot forth your branches,== and yield your fruit to ==My people of Israel;== for they are at hand to come.
Ezek. 36:9 For, behold, I *am* for you, and I will turn unto you, and ==ye shall be tilled and sown:==

"ye shall shoot forth your branches"
When asked for the sign of His return to set up His earthly kingdom, Jesus said:

> **Luke 21:29** ...Behold the fig tree [Israel], and all the trees [nations about which the Prophets spoke];
> **Luke 21:30** When they now shoot forth, ye see and know of your own selves that summer is now nigh at hand.
> **Luke 21:31** So likewise ye, when ye see these things come to pass, know ye that the kingdom of God is nigh at hand.

In other words, when they shoot forth into their prophetic places. The 36th Chapter of Ezekiel is about Israel's return and her "shooting forth" into her prophetic place.

"My people of Israel"
God calls Israel at the time of her return, "My people."
Now is the time of her return, and no one has a right to call them otherwise.

"ye shall be tilled and sown"
When Israel was cast out, it was declared that it would be a waste wilderness and no one could make it bear fruit. The sages said that an evident sign that the time of the Messiah was drawing near, would be that the Land could be tilled and bear fruit again.

> **Lev. 26:32** And I will bring the land into desolation: and your enemies which dwell therein shall be astonished at it.

Is. 27:6 He shall cause them that come of Jacob to take root: Israel shall blossom and bud, and **fill** the face of the world with **fruit**.

Ezek. 36:10 And I will multiply men upon you, all the house of Israel, *even* all of it: and the cities shall be inhabited, and the wastes shall be builded:
Ezek. 36:11 And I will multiply upon you man and beast; and they shall increase and bring fruit: and I will settle you after your old estates, and will do better *unto you* than at your beginnings: and ye shall know that I *am* the LORD.
Ezek. 36:12 Yea, I will cause men to walk upon you, *even* my people Israel; and they shall possess thee, and thou shalt be their inheritance, and thou shalt no more henceforth bereave them of *men*.

"all the house of Israel, all of it"
Both the northern and the southern kingdoms.
The northern kingdom (10 "lost" tribes) conquered and assimilated into Assyria in 722 BC.
And the southern kingdom (Judea) which was completely conquered and the Temple burned by Babylon in 586 BC.

"the cities shall be inhabited, and the wastes shall be builded"
Jews who know this command and obey it have resettled the old cities and estates. The world calls them "West Bank settlements." I cringe when I hear U.S. politicians decry them. Presidents, Statesmen, Ambassadors have scolded Israel for rebuilding them. Often times, they think they are blessing Israel, but they are ignorant of the written Word of God on the matter. They need to study the Bible and a good Bible Atlas to know God's will for the so-called West Bank. Thank God, many believers who know the truth of God's will are praying for America. More believers every day are being enlightened as to God's will concerning Israel.

"My people Israel shall possess thee"
There is no need to debate the issue. God has spoken and it shall surely *"be their inheritance."* No promise is so often repeated in the Scriptures as the promise that the LORD will being 'His people Israel' back to the Land He promised them. Perhaps this is because so many are willing to yield to the enemy of God when he works to stop this Word of the Lord from coming to pass. Satan is ever fighting the Word's fulfillment. In the garden he asked, "Hath God said?"

Ezek. 36:13 Thus saith the Lord GOD; Because they say unto you, Thou *land* devourest up men, and hast bereaved thy nations;
Ezek. 36:14 Therefore thou shalt devour men no more, neither bereave thy nations any more, saith the Lord GOD.
Ezek. 36:15 Neither will I cause *men* to hear in thee the shame of the heathen any more, neither shalt thou bear the reproach of the people any more, neither shalt thou cause thy nations to fall any more, saith the Lord GOD.

Yechezkel, ArtScrolls
Over the centuries *Eretz Yisrael* would come to be known as an inhospitable land...The land became an object of derision; it seemed to consume its inhabitants, to be unable to hold its people.

The cause for this historical phenomenon lies in the land's unique status of being God's portion on earth (Deuteronomy 32:9). As such it cannot and will not tolerate sin within its boundaries (*Ramban*, Leviticus 18:25), and the Torah predicts (Leviticus 18:25,28) that it will vomit out all those who defile its sanctity...The promise of this section is that the future will be different. No more will the land have to defend itself against desecration.

Ezek. 36:19 And I scattered them among the heathen [*goyim*, nations], and they were dispersed through the countries: according to their way and according to their doings I judged them.
Ezek. 36:20 And when they entered unto the heathen, whither they went, they profaned my holy name, when they said to them, These *are* the people of the LORD, and are gone forth out of his land.
Ezek. 36:21 But I had pity for mine holy name, which the house of Israel had profaned among the heathen, whither they went.
Ezek. 36:22 Therefore say unto the house of Israel, Thus saith the Lord GOD; I do not *this* for your sakes, O house of Israel, but for mine holy name's sake, which ye have profaned among the heathen, whither ye went.
Ezek. 36:23 And I will sanctify my great name, which was profaned among the heathen, which ye have profaned in the midst of them; and the heathen shall know that I *am* the LORD, saith the Lord GOD, when I shall be sanctified in you before their eyes.
Ezek. 36:24 For I will take you from among the heathen, and gather you out of all countries, and will bring you into your own land.

God's Dealings with Israel are a key to unlocking Bible Prophecy. We can tell where we are on the time line by knowing what God is doing with this prophetic nation during our lifetime.

God's Dealings with Israel

1. The Choosing
2. The Blessing
3. The Bringing into the Land
4. The Scattering
5. The Ingathering (Bringing back to the Land.)
6. The Restoration
7. The Redemption

"I scattered them" "I will ...gather you...and bring you into your own land."
In verses 19 and 24, we see the scattering and the gathering.
We live in the time of the Ingathering.

"whither they went, they profaned my holy name, when they said to them, These are the people of the LORD (Jehovah), and are gone forth out of His Land."
I have thought about this and personalized it. What if my children or grandchildren were on the streets, homeless, tattered, hungry, and someone recognized them and exclaimed, "These are the children of Billye Brim. Why doesn't she provide for them?"

Remember Plan A and the Blessings were available to Israel. (See Section I, Chapter 3, The Jews, The Nations, and The Church, Israel's Purpose and Call).

"Mine holy name's sake...I will sanctify My holy name"
God's name will be sanctified in all the earth.

Israel's National Cleansing

Ezek. 36:25 Then will I sprinkle clean water upon you, and ye shall be clean: from all your filthiness, and from all your idols, will I cleanse you.
Ezek. 36:26 A new heart also will I give you, and a new spirit will I put within you: and I will take away the stony heart out of your flesh, and I will give you an heart of flesh.
Ezek. 36:27 And I will put my spirit within you, and cause you to walk in my statutes, and ye shall keep my judgments, and do *them.*
Ezek. 36:28 And ye shall dwell in the land that I gave to your fathers; and ye shall be my people, and I will be your God.

These verses speak of the redemption of Israel.

Ezek. 36:33 Thus saith the Lord GOD; ==In the day that I shall have cleansed you== from all your iniquities I will also cause *you* to dwell in the cities, and the wastes shall be builded.
Ezek. 36:34 And the desolate land shall be tilled, whereas it lay desolate in the sight of all that passed by.
Ezek. 36:35 And they shall say, This land that was desolate is become like the garden of Eden; and the waste and desolate and ruined cities *are become* fenced, *and* are inhabited.
Ezek. 36:36 ==Then the heathen that are left round about you shall know== that I the LORD build the ruined *places, and* plant that that was desolate: I the LORD have spoken *it,* and I will do *it.*

"In the day that I shall have cleansed you"
This speaks of the nation as a nation. A national redemption.

> **Jer. 50:20** In those days, and in that time, saith the LORD, the iniquity of Israel [northern kingdom] shall be sought for, and *there shall be* none; and the sins of Judah [southern kingdom], and they shall not be found: for I will pardon them whom I reserve.

Is. 62:12 And they shall call them, The holy people, The redeemed of the LORD: and thou [Jerusalem] shalt be called, Sought out, A city not forsaken.

God's Word Translation
Is. 4:3 Then whoever is left in Zion and whoever remains in Jerusalem will be called holy, everyone who is recorded among the living in Jerusalem.
Is. 4:4 The Lord will wash away the filth of Zion's people. He will clean bloodstains from Jerusalem with a spirit of judgment and a spirit of burning.
Is. 4:5 The Lord will create a cloud of smoke during the day and a glowing flame of fire during the night over the whole area of Mount Zion and over the assembly. His glory will cover everything. [Hebrew: Will be a *choopah*.]

Jer. 31:33 But this *shall be* the covenant that I will make with the house of Israel; After those days, saith the LORD, I will put my law in their inward parts, and write it in their hearts; and will be their God, and they shall be my people.
Jer. 31:34 And they shall teach no more every man his neighbour, and every man his brother, saying, Know the LORD: for they shall all know me, from the least of them unto the greatest of them, saith the LORD: for I will forgive their iniquity, and I will remember their sin no more.

Jer. 31:35 Thus saith the LORD, which giveth the sun for a light by day, *and* the ordinances of the moon and of the stars for a light by night, which divideth the sea when the waves thereof roar; The LORD of hosts *is* his name:
Jer. 31:36 If those ordinances depart from before me, saith the LORD, *then* the seed of Israel also shall cease from being a nation before me for ever.
Jer. 31:37 Thus saith the LORD; If heaven above can be measured, and the foundations of the earth searched out beneath, I will also cast off all the seed of Israel for all that they have done, saith the LORD.

> Israel will be a nation as long as there exist a sun, moon, and stars.
> Israel will be a nation as long as man cannot measure heaven and earth.
>
> Brim note: A very excellent study of this is found in David Baron's *ZECHARIAH, A Commentary on his Visions and Prophecies.* It is too long to go into here, but perhaps this introduction to the last chapters will give you an idea :

> "The overthrow of world-power, and the establishment of Messiah's Kingdom may be given as the epitome of the last six chapters of Zechariah. The two oracles which make up the whole of the second half of the book (chaps. 9-11 and 12-14),...are corresponding portions of a greater whole. Both sections treat of war between the heathen world and Israel, though in different ways.
>
> In the first (chaps 9-11), the judgment through which Gentile world-power over Israel is finally destroyed, and Israel is endowed with the strength to overcome all their enemies... In the second (chaps 12-15), the judgment through which Israel itself is sifted and purged in the final great conflict with the nations, and transformed into the holy nation of Jehovah....

David Baron, *Israel in the Plan of God*, page 118 (Commenting on Deut. 32:43.)

NAS 95
Deut. 32:43
> "Rejoice, O nations, *with* His people;
> For He will avenge the blood of His servants,
> And will render vengeance on His adversaries,
> And will atone for His land *and* His people."

"Rejoice, O nations with His people;"
It is only after "the receiving again" of Israel as a nation that the full tide of universal blessing will come to the world, and that the call will go forth, "Rejoice, O ye nations, with His people." Then the knowledge of the glory of Jehovah shall cover this earth as the waters cover the sea. The saved nations [sheep nations from Matthew 25], together with Israel are to rejoice...

"and will atone for His land and His people."
[the atonement accepted]...will take place when the Spirit of grace and of supplications is poured out on them as a nation...and they mourn... (See Zechariah 12:9 -13:1.)
Of no other land, and of no other people *as a people* [nation], does He speak in the same way. For the land in a very special sense "Immanuel's Land," (Isaiah 8:8), and "Jehovah's portion is His people; Jacob is the lot of His inheritance" (Deut. 32:9).

This, then, is how Jewish history ends [in this age], not in unbelief and apostasy, but in a glorious restoration, to be followed by a national conversion which will be as "life from the dead" (Romans 11:15, 25-27,33-36).

"Then the goyim (nations) that are left round about you shall know"
Again, God reveals Himself to the nations through Israel.
The nations "that are left" could refer to the sheep nations left on earth after the judgment of the nations in Matthew 25.

Ezek. 36:37 Thus saith the Lord GOD; I will yet *for* this be enquired of by the house of Israel, to do *it* for them; I will increase them with men like a flock.
Ezek. 36:38 As the holy flock, as the flock of Jerusalem in her solemn feasts; so shall the waste cities be filled with flocks of men: and they shall know that I *am* the LORD.

> *"I will yet for this be enquired of"*
> Even after long years of exile and wandering, God's covenant with Israel still stands, and she can enquire of Him for it.
>
> *"I will increase them...the waste cities be filled with flocks of men"*
> Though Satan has tried to "swallow up" the Jews from the earth through terrible men and regimes at his disposal, a remnant has returned. However, the promise of the Lord is that there will one day be so many, the land will be too small for them:
>
>> **Is. 49:19** For thy waste and thy desolate places, and the land of thy destruction, shall even now be too narrow by reason of the inhabitants, and they that swallowed thee up shall be far away.
>> **Is. 49:20** The children which thou shalt have, after thou hast lost the other, shall say again in thine ears, The place *is* too strait for me: give place to me that I may dwell.
>
> *"they shall know that I am Jehovah"*
> The recurrent theme of the purposeful God...that men should know that I am Jehovah.

SECTION II

Commentary on The Book of Ezekiel

Ezekiel Chapter 37

The Dry Bones Chapter (The People)

Inspiration of the Spiritual, *Ezekiel Saw the Wheel,* this chapter is about the restoration to fullness of life of the Whole House of Israel.

When someone says "Israel," the word could be referring to either the Land or its people. For Israel is the name of both. In Hebrew it is *Eretz* Israel (the Land) and *Am* Israel (the nation, the people). Chapter 36 is primarily to the Land. Chapter 37 is concerning the People. The Land and the People go together.

Please read the "Dry Bones" portion as a whole. The prophet was transported probably over the Land of Israel.

Ezek. 37:1 The hand of the LORD was upon me, and carried me out in the spirit of the LORD, and set me down in the midst of the valley which *was* full of bones,
Ezek. 37:2 And caused me to pass by them round about: and, behold, *there were* very many in the open valley; and, lo, *they were* very dry.
Ezek. 37:3 And he said unto me, Son of man, can these bones live? And I answered, O Lord GOD, thou knowest.
Ezek. 37:4 Again he said unto me, Prophesy upon these bones, and say unto them, O ye dry bones, hear the word of the LORD.
Ezek. 37:5 Thus saith the Lord GOD unto these bones; Behold, I will cause breath to enter into you, and ye shall live:
Ezek. 37:6 And I will lay sinews upon you, and will bring up flesh upon you, and cover you with skin, and put breath in you, and ye shall live; and ye shall know that I *am* the LORD.
Ezek. 37:7 So I prophesied as I was commanded: and as I prophesied, there was a noise, and behold a shaking, and the bones came together, bone to his bone.
Ezek. 37:8 And when I beheld, lo, the sinews and the flesh came up upon them, and the skin covered them above: but *there was* no breath in them.
Ezek. 37:9 Then said he unto me, Prophesy unto the wind, prophesy, son of man, and say to the wind, Thus saith the Lord GOD; Come from the four winds, O breath, and breathe upon these slain, that they may live.
Ezek. 37:10 So I prophesied as he commanded me, and the breath came into them, and they lived, and stood up upon their feet, an exceeding great army.

Ezek. 37:11 Then he said unto me, Son of man, these bones are the whole house of Israel: behold, they say, Our bones are dried, and our hope is lost: we are cut off for our parts.
Ezek. 37:12 Therefore prophesy and say unto them, Thus saith the Lord GOD; Behold, O my people, I will open your graves, and cause you to come up out of your graves, and bring you into the land of Israel.
Ezek. 37:13 And ye shall know that I *am* the LORD, when I have opened your graves, O my people, and brought you up out of your graves,
Ezek. 37:14 And shall put my spirit in you, and ye shall live, and I shall place you in your own land: then shall ye know that I the LORD have spoken *it,* and performed *it,* saith the LORD.

1:1 *"The Hand of the Lord was upon me,"*
The Hand of the Lord is the Holy Spirit.

37:5 *"breath to enter into you, and you shall live"*
In Hebrew, one word *ruach* is translated into English as three words: spirit, breath, wind.

37:9 *"Come from the four winds, O breath, and breathe upon these slain, that they may live."*
Shulamith Katznelson, founder of the Hebrew language school I attended, gave the best teaching I ever heard on this chapter. As a young woman, she was very much a part of the fighting in the War of Independence. She founded the school just after the Modern State of Israel was declared in May 1948. So she was a witness to the stages of the rebirth of Israel. And she taught the chapter in the order of the restoration: first the bones, then the sinew, then the flesh, then the skin, etc. The final stage she said, as I heard her in the 1980s, was not yet realized. It was to be the entering in of the Spirit into the House of Israel.

37:11 *"These bones are the whole house of Israel."*
This verse is the key to the chapter. There can be no other obscure meaning. And again, it is the whole house, Israel (the northern kingdom) and Judah (the southern kingdom.)

The Union of the Two Sticks: Israel and Judah.

Oh, how pitiful have been the teachings that the sticks are somehow Israel and the Church. The two sticks are who the Bible says they are: Israel and Judah.

"Shadowy meanings" are often attempted with the Scriptures. The Word is to be rightly divided. And some, often influenced by Replacement Theology, whether they realize it or not, give strange interpretations to what is clear in the text.

Consider this description of David Baron, and see why his work is so worthy of study:

Ezekiel Chapter 37

<u>Zechariah</u>, David Baron, Kregal Publications, Grand Rapids, MI Foreword by Walter C. Kaiser, Jr., Academic Dean, and Professor of Semitic Languages and the Old Testament, Trinity Evangelical Divinity School

> "David Baron was born in Russia in 1855 and brought up in a strict, devout Jewish family. His education was under the rigorous tutelage of the Rabbinic training of the period…on a…search of the Scriptures…he found the Messiah to be the Lord Jesus Christ.
>
> "Baron launches right into commenting on Zechariah…He is also ever alert to those places where many in the Gentile Church have 'spiritualized' or even 'phantomised' Scripture when it refers to Jerusalem or Israel. The reader should avoid, warns Baron, substituting an unnatural and shadowy meaning for what is plain and obvious in the text."

So, read it for yourself and see how easy it is to see what the Lord is talking about. The LORD will join again what the sons of Solomon divided into two and He will gather them back to their Land. The prophecy carries on to the Millennial Reign. And Israel is still a nation on the earth before the Lord. God is not through with Israel, as the terrible theology of replacement has perpetrated for almost 2000 years.

Ezek. 37:16 Moreover, thou son of man, take thee one stick, and write upon it, For Judah, and for the children of Israel his companions: then take another stick, and write upon it, For Joseph, the stick of Ephraim, and *for* all the house of Israel his companions:

Ezek. 37:17 And join them one to another into one stick; and they shall become one in thine hand.

Ezek. 37:18 And when the children of thy people shall speak unto thee, saying, Wilt thou not shew us what thou *meanest* by these?

Ezek. 37:19 Say unto them, Thus saith the Lord GOD; Behold, I will take the stick of Joseph, which *is* in the hand of Ephraim, and the tribes of Israel his fellows, and will put them with him, *even* with the stick of Judah, and make them one stick, and they shall be one in mine hand.

Ezek. 37:20 And the sticks whereon thou writest shall be in thine hand before their eyes.

Ezek. 37:21 And say unto them, Thus saith the Lord GOD; Behold, I will take the children of Israel from among the heathen [*goyim*, nations], whither they be gone, and will gather them on every side, and bring them into their own land:

Ezek. 37:22 And I will make them one nation in the land upon the mountains of Israel; and one king shall be king to them all: and they shall be no more two nations, neither shall they be divided into two kingdoms any more at all:

Ezek. 37:23 Neither shall they defile themselves any more with their idols, nor with their detestable things, nor with any of their transgressions: but I will save them out of all their dwelling places, wherein they have sinned, and will cleanse them: so shall they be my people, and I will be their God.

Ezek. 37:24 And David my servant *shall be* king over them; and they all shall have one shepherd: they shall also walk in my judgments, and observe my statutes, and do them.

Ezek. 37:25 And they shall dwell in the land that I have given unto Jacob my servant, wherein your fathers have dwelt; and they shall dwell therein, *even* they, and their children, and their children's children for ever: and my servant David *shall be* their prince for ever.

Ezek. 37:26 Moreover I will make a covenant of peace with them; it shall be an everlasting covenant with them: and I will place them, and multiply them, and will set my sanctuary in the midst of them for evermore.

Ezek. 37:27 My tabernacle also shall be with them: yea, I will be their God, and they shall be my people.

Ezek. 37:28 And the heathen [goyim, nations] shall know that I the LORD do sanctify Israel, when my sanctuary shall be in the midst of them for evermore.

SECTION II

Commentary on The Book of Ezekiel

Chapters 38 and 39

An Invasion of Israel
by the
Forces of Gog

Jewish sages teach that there are two Gog-Magog wars.
I believe there are three distinct wars in the end of days. The first and third are identified with the term Gog and Magog.

    The first: Ezekiel 38, 39
                   (An invasion of Israel by Gog's forces.
                   This war could occur at any time now.)

    The second: Zechariah 14, Revelation 16:16
                   (The Battle of Armageddon.
                   At the end of the Great Tribulation.
                   The Antichrist and his forces.)

    The third: Revelation 20:8
                   (At the end of the 1000 years, Satan is "loosed out
                   of his prison." He goes forth to deceive the nations,
                   Gog and Magog, gathers a large army of followers.
                   God destroys with fire from heaven.)

Psalm 83: I see as an ongoing war of attrition with the forces of Islam against Israel. This war does not have an exact date we can point to as a starting date. It is called by some the Arab-Israeli conflict. But it is really an Islamic confederacy.

Satan – (Hebrew: *adversary*) is the instigator of all. They are his attacks against the plans of God.

Ezek. 38:1 And the word of the LORD came unto me, saying,
Ezek. 38:2 Son of man, set thy face against Gog, the land of Magog, the chief prince of Meshech and Tubal, and prophesy against him,
Ezek. 38:3 And say, Thus saith the Lord GOD; Behold, I *am* against thee, O Gog, the chief prince of Meshech and Tubal:

Gog
I believe Gog is an evil spirit being, Satan. And that he is operating from the mid-heavens, as the prince of the power of the air (Ephesians 2:2), directing the invasion over the city of Moscow.
(See Section II, Chapter 28, and Appendix: *Seat of Satan*.)
It is Gog, the evil Satan, that God is against.

The land of Magog
The earthly area of Gog's operation.

> <u>Yechezkel, ArtScrolls page 580-583</u>
> *Gog of the land of Magog.*
> The various traditions concerning the identity of Magog, who in Genesis 10:2 is listed among the sons of Noah's son, Japheth, tend to place the land of Magog in what today is...Russia...
> Thus...land of Magog, is located in a region aptly described as *the farthest north*...
>
> *Meshech and Tubal,*
> ...both listed in Genesis 10:2 as sons of Japheth...
>
> *prince leader (rosh) of Meshech and Tubal.*
> This salutation...indicates that the *Gaonim* [early Talmudic sages] had a tradition that these countries were indeed located in Russia.

Ezek. 38:5 Persia, Ethiopia, and Libya with them; all of them with shield and helmet:
Ezek. 38:6 Gomer, and all his bands; the house of Togarmah of the north quarters, and all his bands: *and* many people with thee.
Ezek. 38:7 Be thou prepared, and prepare for thyself, thou, and all thy company that are assembled unto thee, and be thou a guard unto them.

Persia - Present day Iran.
A strong alliance between Russia and Iran began with Russia's helping Iran build a nuclear reactor.

> <u>Wikipedia, The On-Line Encyclopedia</u> The **Bushehr Nuclear Power Plant**.
> Construction...was started in 1975 by German companies, but the work was stopped in 1979 after the Islamic revolution of Iran. The site was repeatedly bombed during the Iran–Iraq war. Later, a contract for finishing the plant was signed between Iran and the Russian Ministry for Atomic Energy in 1995.... The work was delayed several years by technical and financial challenges as well as by political pressure from the West. ... The plant ... was officially opened in a ceremony on 12 September 2011....

The evil alliance, which the Lord foresaw, continues until the very time of this writing:

www.defensenews.com

Russia Confirms Sale of S-300 Missile Systems To Iran
MOSCOW — Russia on Tuesday [August 18, 2015] confirmed its decision to deliver S-300 air defense missile systems to Iran....

President Vladimir Putin last month lifted a ban on supplying Iran with the sophisticated systems, following the landmark framework deal Tehran struck with the West over its nuclear program.

More than 2500 years ago, Ezekiel prophesied a Russian-Persian coalition. It is not as if God predestined it; every nation and its leaders have free wills. But by His foreknowledge the Lord sees how things will turn out. His judgments are predicated on their own actions.

Cush and Put – South of Egypt, probably spread over an area which today is the eastern part of the Sudan, Ethiopia, and Eritrea.

Gomer and Togarmah – Son and grandson of Japheth. The *ArtScrolls* commentary states, "Difficult to identify with any certainty."
Josephus (History of the Jews, Ch. 1) identifies the children of Gomer as "the Franks who live in France on the River Seine." The following reference identifies their origin as Germanic tribes.

The Franks, A History of the Franks history-world.org/franks.htm
The Franks were a group of Germanic tribes that, about the middle of the 3rd century AD, dwelt along the middle and lower Rhine River. The Franks appeared in the Roman provinces around 253....

Agreeing with ArtScrolls, that no one can be sure about *Gomer*, I would hazard a guess that they are European. A clue to me is the name of another of Gomer's grandsons, *Ashkenaz*. The Jews from Europe are called *Ashkenazi's*.

Togarmah – Many prophecy teachers teach that *Togarmah* is Turkey.

Wikipedia
Togarmah (Hebrew: תוגרמה) is a figure in the "table of nations" in Genesis 10, the list of descendants of Noah that represents the peoples known to the ancient Hebrews. Togarmah is among the descendants of Japheth and is thought to represent some people located in Anatolia.

Anatolia
Anatolia, in geography known as Asia Minor, Asian Turkey, Anatolian peninsula, or Anatolian plateau, denotes the westernmost protrusion of Asia, which makes up the majority of the Republic of Turkey.

Ezek. 38:8 After many days thou shalt be visited: in the latter years thou shalt come into the land *that is* brought back from the sword, *and is* gathered out of many people, against the mountains of Israel, which have been always waste: but it is brought forth out of the nations, and they shall dwell safely all of them.

The *ArtScroll* translation, I believe, is more accurate. And the commentary on "From ancient times," is telling.

<u>Yechezkel, ArtScrolls, page 585</u>
From ancient times you are to be recalled. In the end of years you shall come to a land restored from the sword, gathered from many nations,...

> *ArtScrolls Commentary*
> *From ancient times [lit. from many days] you are to be recalled.*
> In the *nifal*, [passive] usually means that one is recalled with the purpose of subjecting him to his predestined fate, good or bad.
> *Rashi* sees the wars of *Mashiach ben Yosef* as a time of reckoning for all the evils, which the nations had perpetrated against Israel over the centuries. He renders, You are to be recalled (that is, punished) for sins which were committed long ago.
> ...another interpretation is possible. God's consideration, of Gog goes back into antiquity. This final confrontation...is a culmination of all of world history which was inexorably flowing towards this point; although we could not understand how while the events were taking place (*R Breuer*).

<u>Brim Note:</u> I have studied what is called Anti-Semitism throughout history. And this commentary brings to my mind more recent history of terrible atrocities perpetrated against the Jews from these very geographical areas. As mentioned, however, it probably goes back into antiquity as well.

"against the mountains of Israel, which have been always waste: but it is brought forth out of the nations."
See Ezekiel 36. At the time of the Ingathering.

Ezek. 38:9 Thou shalt ascend and come like a storm, thou shalt be like a cloud to cover the land, thou, and all thy bands, and many people with thee.

An attack from the air.

Ezek. 38:10 Thus saith the Lord GOD; It shall also come to pass, *that* at the same time shall things come into thy mind, and thou shalt think an evil thought:
Ezek. 38:11 And thou shalt say, I will go up to the land of unwalled villages; I will go to them that are at rest, that dwell safely, all of them dwelling without walls, and having neither bars nor gates,

In Bible times important cities had walls. It was not until the resettlement of Israel in very recent times that Jews began to live outside walls. And to build towns without walls. I believe the Prophet was referring to the time when things would have changed:

Mishkenot She'ananim –The First Settlement Outside The Old City Walls:

Until the middle of the 19th century, all the people of Jerusalem lived inside the Old City Walls. Different ethnic groups: Muslims, Jews, Christians and Armenians lived together in an area of only one square kilometer. Being outside the City walls was considered very dangerous, especially at night. People were scared of being attacked by gangs of robbers and only felt safe inside the city walls. Accordingly, the old city became overcrowded. Living in such crowded conditions was hazardous for everyone's health. Diseases spread quickly among the old city's residents because it was hard to be hygienic under such conditions. People were also incredibly poor because there were not enough job opportunities for them. It was clear that the only solution for the city's natural growth was to build new neighborhoods outside the old city walls....

Moses Montifiore was a wealthy English Jew who decided to help the Jewish community inside the old city walls by buying lands outside the old city walls. Montifiore decided to...create a new settlement outside the city walls for Torah scholars who were poor and needy.

In the year 1860, Moses Montifiore built the first settlement outside of the walls. He named the neighborhood Mishkenot Sheananim....

Poor Torah Scholars and their families quickly populated Mishkenot Sheananim. At the beginning they were frightened to sleep outside the old city walls, so they would return to their original homes to sleep at night. (Wikipedia)

Ezek. 38:12 To take a spoil, and to take a prey; to turn thine hand upon the desolate places *that are now* inhabited, and upon the people *that are* gathered out of the nations, which have gotten cattle and goods, that dwell in the midst of the land.

Ezek. 38:13 Sheba, and Dedan, and the merchants of Tarshish, with all the young lions thereof, shall say unto thee, Art thou come to take a spoil? hast thou gathered thy company to take a prey? to carry away silver and gold, to take away cattle and goods, to take a great spoil?

> *To take a spoil....*
> Some prophecy teachers have said it would be "oil."
> This would take a "supernatural" discovery.
> I really don't know what the "spoil" is, but the Word of God declares it, so it shall surely be.
>
> <u>*Sheba and Dedan and the merchants of Tarshish, with all the young lions thereof,*</u>
> Sheba and Dedan were sons of Keturah who became forefathers of the Arabs:
>
> > **1 Chr. 1:32** Now the sons of **Keturah**, Abraham's concubine: she bare Zimran, and Jokshan, and Medan, and Midian, and Ishbak, and Shuah. And the sons of Jokshan; Sheba, and Dedan.

Dr. Hilton Sutton, a mentor and friend, believed Sheba and Dedan were perhaps Saudi Arabia — and that the young lions of the merchants of Tarshish, who were sailors, could include England, and her offspring, the United States.

He put forth his idea that when the invading armies came down into Israel, these other nations might hold a press conference in which they asked the questions posed in verse 13. Whimsically, he inferred that might be all they did about it.

Ezek. 38:15 And thou shalt come from thy place out of the north parts, thou, and many people with thee, all of them riding upon horses, a great company, and a mighty army:
Ezek. 38:16 And thou shalt come up against my people of Israel, as a cloud to cover the land; it shall be in the latter days [the end of days], and I will bring thee against my land, that ==the heathen [*goyim,* nations] may know me, when I shall be sanctified in thee, O Gog, before their eyes.==

> *"out of the north parts"*
> *ArtScrolls* translates this, *"from your place in the farthest north."*
> Moscow is due north from Jerusalem.
>
> *"My people Israel"*
> This will occur in the end of days and God calls them, "My people Israel." Would that politicians and all people might recognize Israel's status as the apple of God's eye, and be on the Lord's side concerning them.
>
> *"as a cloud to cover the land..."*
> Throughout the prophecy, the prophet uses the only terms he knew at the time to describe an invading army he could not even imagine.
>
> *"it shall be in the end of days"*
> The time is fixed. It could only happen now when we live. Considering the current alignment of nations, *we could see it happen at any time.*
>
> *"I will bring thee..."*
> God brings them down for His purposes....
>
> ==*"that the nations may know me, when I shall be sanctified in thee, O Gog, before their eyes..."*==
> Throughout the prophecy, God sets forth this as His purpose.
> I believe that the nations around about will recognize that it is a supernatural victory evidently brought forth by the Hand of Israel's God, Jehovah.
> And that there will be recognition by Israel's Islamic neighbors that Jehovah is God. I believe many Muslims, and others, will turn to Jehovah God. I believe that this short, supernatural victory will result in a huge number of surrounding peoples coming to God. Muslims in particular.
>
> Israel, too, will recognize Jehovah in this victory:
>
>> **Ezek. 39:7** So will I make my holy name known in the midst of my people Israel; and I will not *let them* pollute my holy name any more: and the heathen [nations] shall know that I *am* the LORD, the Holy One in Israel.

ASV 95
Ezek. 38:18 "It will come about on that day, when Gog comes against the land of Israel," declares the Lord GOD, "that My fury will mount up in My anger.
Ezek. 38:19 "In My zeal and in My blazing wrath I declare *that* on that day there will surely be a great earthquake in the land of Israel.
Ezek. 38:20 "The fish of the sea, the birds of the heavens, the beasts of the field, all the creeping things that creep on the earth, and all the men who are on the face of the earth will shake at My presence; the mountains also will be thrown down, the steep pathways will collapse and every wall will fall to the ground.
Ezek. 38:21 "I will call for a sword against him on all My mountains," declares the Lord GOD. "Every man's sword will be against his brother.
Ezek. 38:22 "With pestilence and with blood I will enter into judgment with him; and I will rain on him and on his troops, and on the many peoples who are with him, a torrential rain, with hailstones, fire and brimstone.
Ezek. 38:23 ==I will magnify Myself, sanctify Myself, and make Myself known in the sight of many nations; and they will know that I am the LORD.==

> Brim Note: The following scripture, I believe, could relate to Ezekiel 38 and 39 — particularly verse 14, which speaks of "them that spoil us." If it does, God's supernatural forces will result in a quick easy-to-see-it-is Jehovah victory.
>
> > **Is. 17:12** Woe to the multitude of many people, *which* make a noise like the noise of the seas; and to the rushing of nations, *that* make a rushing like the rushing of mighty waters!
> > **Is. 17:13** The nations shall rush like the rushing of many waters: but *God* shall rebuke them, and they shall flee far off, and shall be chased as the chaff of the mountains before the wind, and like a rolling thing before the whirlwind.
> > **Is. 17:14** And behold at eveningtide trouble; *and* before the morning he *is* not. This *is* the portion of them that spoil us, and the lot of them that rob us.
>
> Isaiah 17 is the "Burden of Damascus" chapter which says, "Damascus is taken away from being a city, and it shall be a ruinous heap" (Isaiah 17:1). I have long seen that Syria is not listed in Ezekiel 38 as an ally in this invasion — even in the light of how long Russia and Syria have been cohorts.
> So, I thought Damascus would be wiped out in some sort of limited nuclear blast, probably at the hands of Israel.
>
> But recent developments in the "Syrian Civil War," at this writing, have virtually crippled the Syrian regime of the Assad's. Various groups are fighting for the territory we have known as Syria.
>
> When you read this, it may all be sorted out. But at any rate Syria, as it was known in the 20th and early 21st Centuries, is not the same.

Ezekiel Chapter 39
The Invasion Continued

This chapter continues the invasion and the immediate aftermath. My comments are on only a few verses.

KJV
Ezek. 39:2 And I will turn thee back, and leave but the sixth part of thee, and will cause thee to come up from the north parts, and will bring thee upon the mountains of Israel:

This verse is perplexing to translate. The challenge is a certain word, the meaning of which could be taken two ways. One, meaning to *seduce* or *persuade*. The other could relate to the word for *six*.

Yechezkel, ArtScrolls
I shall lead you astray and seduce you, and I shall cause you to advance from the farthest north and bring you to the mountains of Israel...

> ArtScrolls note:
> *Radak* suggests that it means to destroy, or that it is related to six: I will reduce you to a sixth [of your population]...

Amplified Bible
Ezek. 39:2 And I will turn you about and will lead you on, and will cause you to come up from the uttermost parts of the north and will lead you against the mountains of Israel;

Young's Literal Translation
Ezek. 39:2 And have turned thee back, and enticed thee, And caused thee to come up from the sides of the north, And brought thee in against mountains of Israel,

Ezek. 39:9 And they that dwell in the cities of Israel shall go forth, and shall set on fire and burn the weapons, both the shields and the bucklers, the bows and the arrows, and the handstaves, and the spears, and ==they shall burn them with fire seven years:==

This relatively long period seems to indicate to me that the war *could* happen at any time. Verses 11-16 *may* also indicate a relatively "normal" period rather than the tribulation time, for instance. I emphasize "may" because no one can say for sure. Also worth noting is that seven years is a *schmittah* cycle. And again, nothing in the scripture says this seven years is a *schmittah* cycle.

KJV
Ezek. 39:11 And it shall come to pass in that day, *that* I will give unto Gog a place there of graves in Israel, the valley of the ==passengers== on the east of the sea: and it shall stop the *noses* of the passengers: and there shall they bury Gog and all his multitude: and they shall call *it* The valley of Hamongog.

Ezek. 39:12 And seven months shall the house of Israel be burying of them, that they may cleanse the land.
Ezek. 39:13 Yea, all the people of the land shall bury *them;* and it shall be to them a renown the day that I shall be glorified, saith the Lord GOD.
Ezek. 39:14 And they shall sever out men of continual employment, passing through the land to bury with the passengers those that remain upon the face of the earth, to cleanse it: after the end of seven months shall they search.
Ezek. 39:15 And the passengers *that* pass through the land, when *any* seeth a man's bone, then shall he set up a sign by it, till the buriers have buried it in the valley of Hamongog.
Ezek. 39:16 And also the name of the city *shall be* Hamonah. Thus shall they cleanse the land.

Passengers
May mean just "those passing by," but could it mean tourists?

Seven months
The number seven is always significant

Cleanse the land
The Holy Land is to be cleansed of all traces of death.
A friend of mine was a policeman in Netanya when the terrible Beit Lid tragedy occurred at a bus stop where soldiers were standing. He told me how the special Jewish religious task force literally scraped remains of human flesh off lampposts, etc., so that the area could be cleansed.

> *Wikipedia*
> The **Beit Lid suicide bombing**...was a suicide attack by Palestinian Islamic Jihad against Israeli soldiers at the Beit Lid Junction on January 22, 1995. It was the first suicide attack by Palestinian Islamic Jihad....
> at approximately 9:30 am, a Palestinian suicide bomber, disguised as an Israeli soldier, approached the bus stop at the Beit Lid junction in central Israel. The bus stop was full of Israeli soldiers who were on their way to their bases after their weekend vacation. The suicide bomber walked into the crowd and detonated the hidden explosives belt he was wearing. About three minutes later a second suicide bomber exploded at the same spot, killing and injuring people wounded in the first explosion, as well as bystanders who had rushed to the scene to assist the victims of the first explosion.

Ezek. 39:17 And, thou son of man, thus saith the Lord GOD; Speak unto every feathered fowl, and to every beast of the field, Assemble yourselves, and come; gather yourselves on every side to my sacrifice that I do sacrifice for you, *even* a great sacrifice upon the mountains of Israel, that ye may eat flesh, and drink blood.
Ezek. 39:18 Ye shall eat the flesh of the mighty, and drink the blood of the princes of the earth, of rams, of lambs, and of goats, of bullocks, all of them fatlings of Bashan.
Ezek. 39:19 And ye shall eat fat till ye be full, and drink blood till ye be drunken, of my sacrifice which I have sacrificed for you.

Ezek. 39:20 Thus ye shall be filled at my table with horses and chariots, with mighty men, and with all men of war, saith the Lord GOD.

> When Israel gave up the Sinai to Egypt, their air space was drastically reduced. Israel today is the size of the State of New Jersey — only 60 miles wide at its widest point. If you put the bottommost part of Israel on Los Angeles, its top would not quite reach San Francisco. As a result, Israel's flight training space was dangerously worsened. They lost more planes to birds than to enemy fire.
>
> Consider the three-leaved ancient map we included elsewhere. Israel (most people when asked cannot identify the continent Israel is on; it is Asia) is a land bridge between three continents: Europe, Asia, and Africa. It not only was the easiest passageway for ancient armies and trade caravans — it is the easiest pathway for large birds. During migration seasons (spring and autumn), large birds ride the thermals over Israel to their destinations, either north or south.
>
> The Israelis studied the problem and discovered they could predict to the day the travel of the birds. And they solved their problem accordingly.
>
> I believe the prophet Ezekiel summoned the birds (39:17). They are already invited to the feast. Certain Rabbis therefore believe this battle will take place in the autumn. Spring is also a possibility.
>
> The battle called Armageddon, during which the King Messiah comes to earth on his white horse, also mentions the feast for the birds (Revelation 19:16). So we have a clue to its' timing as well. And this one, I believe, will be in the autumn at the time of the high holy days, usually in September or October. For it will be at the end of the seven-year *schmittah* cycle of both the marriage supper of the Lamb in heaven, and of the tribulation period on earth.

Ezek. 39:21 And I will set my glory among the heathen [goyim, nations], and all the heathen shall see my judgment that I have executed, and my hand that I have laid upon them.
Ezek. 39:22 So the house of Israel shall know that I am the LORD their God from that day and forward.

> *God's purpose: to reveal Himself.*
> *To the nations:* He is revealed through His dealings with Israel.
> *To the House of Israel:* Many people in Israel are secular. Some believe, but are not "practicing." Others even claim to be atheists. Some say they lost their faith when the holocaust happened. In verse 22, from that day forward, they will know that He is Jehovah their God.

The Ingathering

Ezek. 39:25 Therefore thus saith the Lord GOD; Now will I bring again the captivity of Jacob, and have mercy upon the whole house of Israel, and will be jealous for my holy name;

Ezek. 39:26 After that they have borne their shame, and all their trespasses whereby they have trespassed against me, when they dwelt safely in their land, and none made *them* afraid.

Ezek. 39:27 When I have brought them again from the people, and gathered them out of their enemies' lands, and am sanctified in them in the sight of many nations;

Ezek. 39:28 Then shall they know that I *am* the LORD their God, which caused them to be led into captivity among the heathen [*goyim,* nations]: but I have gathered them unto their own land, and have left none of them any more there.

Ezek. 39:29 Neither will I hide my face any more from them: for I have poured out my spirit upon the house of Israel, saith the Lord GOD.

SECTION II

Commentary on The Book of Ezekiel

Ezekiel Chapters 40 - 48

The Millennial Temple
and
Israel in the Millennium

Chapters 40 through 48 are prophetical of the Millennium.
The Seventh One Thousand Year Day.

Chapter 40

Ezek. 40:2 In the visions of God brought he me into the land of Israel, and set me upon a very high mountain, by which *was* as the frame of a city on the south.
Ezek. 40:3 And he brought me thither, and, behold, *there was* a man, whose appearance *was* like the appearance of brass, with a line of flax in his hand, and a measuring reed; and he stood in the gate.
Ezek. 40:4 And the man said unto me, Son of man, behold with thine eyes, and hear with thine ears, and set thine heart upon all that I shall shew thee; for to the intent that I might shew *them* unto thee *art* thou brought hither: declare all that thou seest to the house of Israel.

> A heavenly being is sent to measure the Temple. That signifies the certainty of its being built. This encouraging vision comes for a people who have known the destruction of the First Temple. The size of the Temple is beyond anything they could have imagined. Indeed, it is the Temple of the Millennial Reign of the King Messiah.
>
> I believe the Jews will build the third Temple (which the antichrist will desecrate). The King Messiah will build the Millennial Temple according to these magnificent plans.

Chapter 43
The Shechinah Glory Returns

Ezek. 43:1 Afterward he brought me to the gate, *even* the gate that looketh toward the east:
Ezek. 43:2 And, behold, the glory of the God of Israel came from the way of the east: and his voice *was* like a noise of many waters: and the earth shined with his glory.

Ezek. 43:3 And *it was* according to the appearance of the vision which I saw, *even* according to the vision that I saw when I came to destroy the city: and the visions *were* like the vision that I saw by the river Chebar; and I fell upon my face.
Ezek. 43:4 And the glory of the LORD came into the house by the way of the gate whose prospect *is* toward the east.
Ezek. 43:5 So the spirit took me up, and brought me into the inner court; and, behold, the glory of the LORD filled the house.

His Presence to be With Israel Forever

Ezek. 43:7 And he said unto me, Son of man, the place of my throne, and the place of the soles of my feet, where I will dwell in the midst of the children of Israel for ever, and my holy name, shall the house of Israel no more defile,

Chapter 45
The Apportionment of the Land

Ezek. 45:1 Moreover, when ye shall divide by lot the land for inheritance, ye shall offer an oblation unto the LORD, an holy portion of the land: the length *shall be* the length of five and twenty thousand *reeds*, and the breadth *shall be* ten thousand. This *shall be* holy in all the borders thereof round about.
Ezek. 45:2 Of this there shall be for the sanctuary five hundred *in length*, with five hundred *in breadth*, square round about; and fifty cubits round about for the suburbs thereof.

Ezek. 45:7 And a *portion shall be* for the prince on the one side and on the other side of the oblation of the holy *portion*, and of the possession of the city, before the oblation of the holy *portion*, and before the possession of the city, from the west side westward, and from the east side eastward: and the length *shall be* over against one of the portions, from the west border unto the east border.
Ezek. 45:8 In the land shall be his possession in Israel: and my princes shall no more oppress my people; and *the rest of* the land shall they give to the house of Israel according to their tribes.

> There is no doubt about who inherits the Land of Israel.
> It is certainly not the church.
> The home and governmental center of the Jews is earthly Jerusalem.
> The home and governmental center of the Church is heavenly Jerusalem.
> (Philippians 3:20. And see my Syllabus on the Book of Revelation.)

Chapter 45:13 – Chapter 46
Reestablishment of Offerings at the Feasts.
Sabbaths and New Moons.

> Why this is, one can only guess. My guess is that the majority of the people on the earth at that time are Gentiles (*goyim*). These nations have made it

into the Millennium on a works judgment after the judgment of the nations of Matthew 25. They are the sheep nations. They are not new creatures. Perhaps they have to learn from the same types of the Old Testament. But this is only a guess.

Chapter 47
The Living Waters

Ezek. 47:1 Afterward he brought me again unto the door of the house; and, behold, waters issued out from under the threshold of the house eastward: for the forefront of the house *stood toward* the east, and the waters came down from under from the right side of the house, at the south *side* of the altar.

> This is one of my favorite prophetic chapters.
> Be sure to read all of it in your Bible.
> Every time I go to Israel, and drive from The Temple Mount area down to what we call The Dead Sea (the Bible calls it The Salt Sea), visions of this future event come to my mind.

> Ezekiel describes these waters flowing from the Temple.
> The heaven-sent messenger measures distances and depths of the waters.
> First the waters are ankle deep.
> Then knee deep.
> Then to the loins.
> Then a river, waters to swim in:

Ezek. 47:5 Afterward he measured a thousand; *and it was* a river that I could not pass over: for the waters were risen, waters to swim in, a river that could not be passed over.

> These waters are living. When they reach the salty waters where there is no life, those waters will be healed. The Dead Sea shall become a Sea of Life!

Ezek. 47:8 Then said he unto me, These waters issue out toward the east country, and go down into the desert, and go into the sea: *which being* brought forth into the sea, the waters shall be healed.
Ezek. 47:9 And it shall come to pass, *that* every thing that liveth, which moveth, whithersoever the rivers shall come, shall live: and there shall be a very great multitude of fish, because these waters shall come thither: for they shall be healed; and every thing shall live whither the river cometh.

> When I am driving with a busload of our seminar students, I get so thrilled when we pass Engedi. I know the very spot where waters flow into the Salt Sea from the hills of Engedi where David and his men camped, and where they probably bathed in the waterfalls high in the mountains. Of course, now when they enter the Sea, they turn to salt waters. I always point to this spot and confidently predict that it will one day be a hot fishing spot.

Ezek. 47:10 And it shall come to pass, *that* the fishers shall stand upon it from Engedi even unto Eneglaim; they shall be a *place* to spread forth nets; their fish shall be according to their kinds, as the fish of the great sea, exceeding many.

The Leaves of the Trees For Healing

Ezek. 47:12 And by the river upon the bank thereof, on this side and on that side, shall grow all trees for meat, whose leaf shall not fade, neither shall the fruit thereof be consumed: it shall bring forth new fruit according to his months, because their waters they issued out of the sanctuary: and the fruit thereof shall be for meat, and the leaf thereof for medicine.

> Perhaps there will not be sickness and disease in the Millennium. For sure the devil will be in the pit. However, I suppose one could still have an accident, etc. For the leaves of these trees are "for medicine."
> (Maybe the leaves can be ground and bottled and shipped around the world so the biblical Millennials can get them without going to The Holy Land. Or maybe they go there in Millennial vehicles that can travel at unimaginable speeds to pick them off the trees. *Just my musings.*)

> Earth is a mirror image of heaven. There is an earthly Jerusalem. There is a heavenly Jerusalem. This earthly river and the trees along its banks are a reflection of a heavenly river.
>
>> **Rev. 22:1** And he shewed me a pure river of water of life, clear as crystal, proceeding out of the throne of God and of the Lamb.
>> **Rev. 22:2** In the midst of the street of it, and on either side of the river, *was there* the tree of life, which bare twelve *manner* of fruits, *and* yielded her fruit every month: and the leaves of the tree *were* for the healing of the nations.

Chapter 47:13 – Chapter 48:29
Detailed Division of the Land

Ezek. 47:13 Thus saith the Lord GOD; This *shall be* the border, whereby ye shall inherit the land according to the twelve tribes of Israel: Joseph *shall have two* portions.
Ezek. 47:14 And ye shall inherit it, one as well as another: *concerning* the which I lifted up mine hand to give it unto your fathers: and this land shall fall unto you for inheritance.

Ezek. 47:21 So shall ye divide this land unto you according to the tribes of Israel.

> No question about it. The Land goes to the twelve tribes of Israel.

> Verse 14. Another instance, there are many, of the fact that God lifted His hand, so to speak, in an oath that Israel gets the Land.

Ezek. 47:15 And this *shall be* the border of the land toward the north side...
Ezek. 47:16 Hamath, Berothah, Sibraim, which *is* between the border of Damascus and the border of Hamath; Hazarhatticon, which *is* by the coast of Hauran.
Ezek. 47:17 And the border from the sea shall be Hazarenan, the border of Damascus, and the north northward, and the border of Hamath. And *this is* the north side.

> The Millennial Land will be much larger than present day Israel.

Ezek. 47:22 And it shall come to pass, *that* ye shall divide it by lot for an inheritance unto you, and to the strangers that sojourn among you, which shall beget children among you: and they shall be unto you as born in the country among the children of Israel; they shall have inheritance with you among the tribes of Israel.
Ezek. 47:23 And it shall come to pass, *that* in what tribe the stranger sojourneth, there shall ye give *him* his inheritance, saith the Lord GOD.

> Provision is made for the strangers within their gates.
> These strangers will be there because they recognize Israel and have blessed it. It would be so wonderful today if people would encourage the so-called Palestinians to recognize what God is doing, and His plan for Israel. They could know the blessings of Genesis 12:3. Here we have the biblical assurance that other nations can and will know blessing in Israel.

Chapter 48

Ezek. 48:1 Now these *are* the names of the tribes. From the north end to the coast of the way of Hethlon, as one goeth to Hamath, Hazarenan, the border of Damascus northward, to the coast of Hamath; for these are his sides east *and* west; a *portion for* Dan....

Ezek. 48:29 This *is* the land which ye shall divide by lot unto the tribes of Israel for inheritance, and these *are* their portions, saith the Lord GOD.

> Further on the distribution of the Land among the tribes.
> Though Dan is not mentioned in Revelation as being represented in the 144,00, the tribe is definitely still recognized in the Millennial distribution of Land. And the Millennium is after the tribulation period of Revelation.

The Gates of the Holy City
Named for the Twelve Tribes

Ezek. 48:31 And the gates of the city *shall be* after the names of the tribes of Israel: three gates northward; one gate of Reuben, one gate of Judah, one gate of Levi.
Ezek. 48:32 And at the east side four thousand and five hundred: and three gates; and one gate of Joseph, one gate of Benjamin, one gate of Dan.
Ezek. 48:33 And at the south side four thousand and five hundred measures: and three gates; one gate of Simeon, one gate of Issachar, one gate of Zebulun.

Ezek. 48:34 At the west side four thousand and five hundred, *with* their three gates; one gate of Gad, one gate of Asher, one gate of Naphtali.

The Dimensions of Jerusalem
The Eternal City

And the Name of the City from that Day

Ezek. 48:35 *It was* round about eighteen thousand *measures:* and the name of the city from *that* day *shall be,* The LORD *is* there.

Jehovah Shammah

THE LORD IS THERE

Study Syllabus for
The Book of Ezekiel

Appendix

Seven Days Chart of Years	106
Table of Nations	107
Map of Israel	108
Three Leaf Ancient Map	109
Arab vs Israel State Comparison	109
The Amazing Ezekiel Stones - Article by David A. Lewis	110
Photos of Ezekiel Stones	113
Mother of the Pound - Excerpts from the book by David Kazzaz	114
Image from Nebuchadnezzar's Dream	117
Babylonian Empire Map	118
Persian Empire Map	118
Quotes from, The Wars of the Jews, by Flavius Josephus	119
Tyre, The Destruction of - Article from the internet	120
Seat of Satan - Article by Billye Brim	122

Seven Days Chart of Years

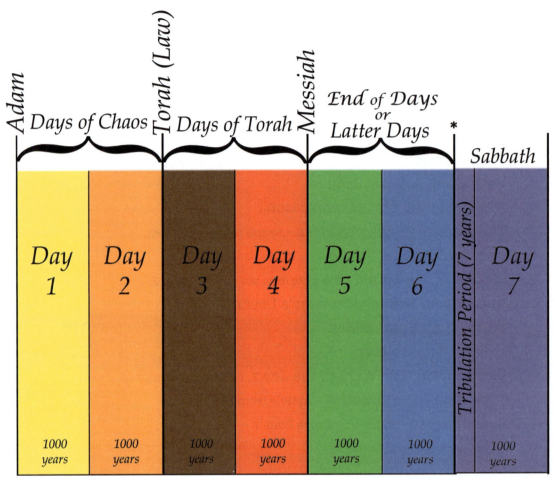

*The 7-year schmittah cycle known as the time of both the Marriage Supper of the Lamb and The Tribulation period could come at the end of the sixth day, or the beginning of the seventh day.

THE TABLE OF THE NATIONS
ACCORDING TO GENESIS 10
FROM THE 3 SONS OF NOAH: SHEM, HAM, AND JAPETH

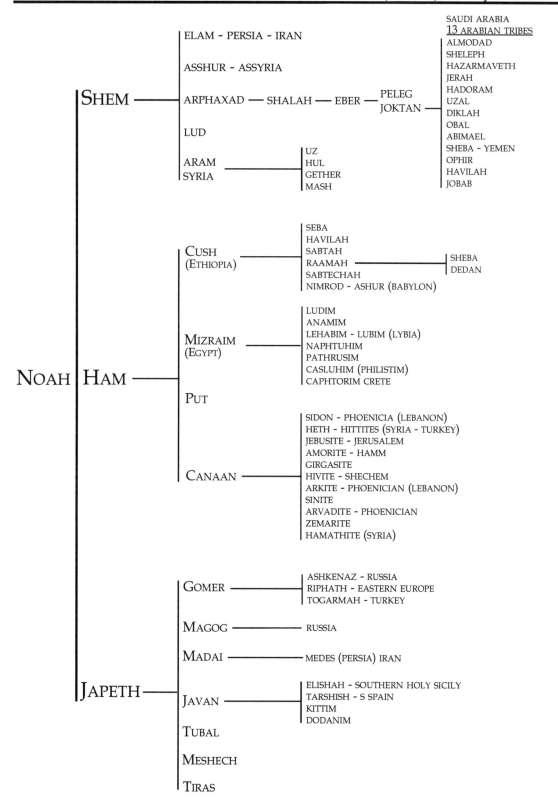

Topographical Map of Israel
Source: www.freeworldmaps.net

Note from freeworldmaps.net: [Maps] are free for any use, even commercial, in the following condition: The exact URL where the original map comes from must be mentioned.

Appendix 109

Ancient Three Leafed Map
Shows Strategic Location of Israel - Land bridge between three continents

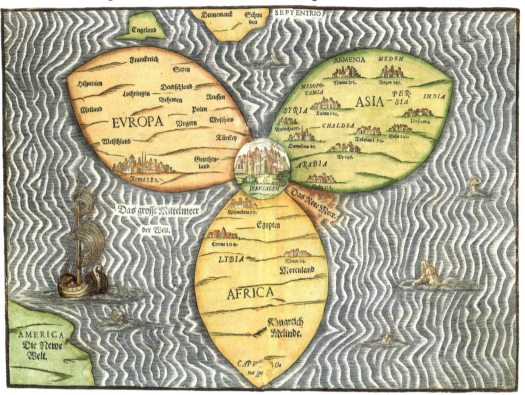

ARABIC STATES **JEWISH STATE**

Arabic - Jewish State Comparison

The Mountains of Israel
The Bible & the West Bank
by Norma Parrish Archbold
Used by Permission

The Amazing Ezekiel Tablets
Article by Dr. David A. Lewis

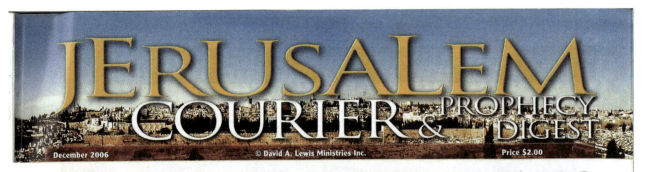

THE AMAZING EZEKIEL TABLETS

In This Issue...

The Amazing Ezekiel Tablets 1-3
Giving Honor Where Honor is Due . .4
Feinstein Challenge 5-8
Book Order Form 9
Audio Tape Order Form 10
Books Available this Month 11-12

Christmas Special

Three Great Books
Written by David Lewis

In these three books you will learn the great truths of Christ's second coming and the part that Israel plays in these end-times events.

Order Your Christmas Special on page 9

Just suppose that somewhere in the Holy Land there is a manuscript of one of the books of the Bible that is so ancient there could be no older copy of that Book, simply because it is the original - from the hand of the prophet himself. There are researchers, in Israel, who believe that they have found the original book of Ezekiel! It is engraved on stone tablets. Is this possible? Here is much of the evidence. If this theory can be proven and brought to public light it will be the most astounding archaeological discovery of all time. *It could either authenticate the text of our modern Bible, or tend to discredit it.* Up until this generation there has been no hint that the actual, original text of one of the books of the Bible might still be in existence. Until now the oldest known manuscript has been one of the Dead Sea Scrolls, dating to about 250 BC (BCE). This would be a manuscript prepared 350 years after the original document. Actually, our Bible is based on copies of copies of copies of the original, unless there is one possible exception. Here are excerpts from my out-of-print book, *The Ezekiel Apocalypse* (which is now a part of a bigger book called *Mysteries of the Bible Now Revealed*), outlining the story of the Ezekiel Tablets, an account of epic proportions.

Many years ago, I met a man named Shlomo Rosenbaum pseudonym used at his request, (for security reasons). He told me that in a secret, highly secured room on the west side of Jerusalem there were sixty-four marble and four basalt tablets each

Ezekiel Tablets See page 2

The Amazing Ezekiel Tablets (continued)
Article by Dr. David A. Lewis (Page 2 of 3)

Ezekiel Tablets from page 1

about fourteen inches square. Written upon these stone tablets was the Book of Ezekiel in the original Hebrew language. There came a day when Shlomo showed me pictures of the mystical Ezekiel stones. Now I can report that I have many slide pictures and many color print pictures; which I took myself, on location.

A band of desert brigands had found the stones in the ancient tomb of the prophet Ezekiel in the village of El Keffil, very near the ruins of the ancient city of Babylon, in the country known today as Iraq. The Ezekiel stones were carried by the grave robbers to Syria, where they passed into the possession of a pharmacist who practiced medicine.

The chieftain of the robber band had become very ill. He told the pharmacist that if he could cure his sickness, he would give him a great archaeological treasure. Little did he realize what a treasure he was being offered. The pharmacist treated the sheik successfully. The grateful desert dweller kept his promise and handed the mystery stones over to the pharmacist. The pharmacist died, never knowing the true nature, nor the value of the treasure he had in his possession.

After his death the stones became the sole property of his grieving widow, a wealthy Christian Arab lady living in the Syrian city of Damascus. She told a religious authority about the stones. He was eager to see them. Upon examination, he said that these stones have the Book of Ezekiel written on them in Hebrew and that he thought they were something very important. He also told her that someday the Ezekiel tablets should become the possession of the Jewish people. At that time the nation of Israel had not yet come into existence as a modern State.

Shlomo obtained funds from a

Jewish sponsor to build the small secure room where the stones are currently standing on a rack available for study by scientists, archeologists, historians, and linguists. For this reason he has had continued access to them, even though he has no official position with the foundation that now has a legitimate claim to ownership of the stone treasure.

After some years had gone by, Shlomo decided to let me come along to see and to photograph the Ezekiel stones. To my amazement, they were unlike any stones with words upon them that I had ever seen. The letters on the Ezekiel tiles leap out from the stone or stand away from the stone in bas-relief fashion. As far as I have been able to discover so far, there is no other example of any extensive ancient writing in existence that uses this style of stone carving. One can find both ancient and modern monuments that feature words displayed in a large —-raised letter style, but there is nothing like the Ezekiel stones. As a matter of fact, Shlomo says that it is a mystery to the researchers working on the Ezekiel project as to how this unique feature was accomplished.

If Shlomo and his associates are ever able to prove their theory concerning the originality of the stones, it will be one of the greatest, if not the greatest archaeological discovery of all time. Remember that our Bibles today are based on copies of copies of copies. No original manuscript of any book of the Bible is in existence as far as we know, unless it is the Ezekiel stones.

The Ezekiel Stones hold hidden clues about the location of Temple treasures such as the lost Ark of the Covenant. When the *Bible Codes* researchers (Moshe Katz, Elayahu Rips, Michael Drosnin, etc.) become aware of the stones they will search for the hidden messages and find information beyond compare!

There is a theory that the Temple of Ezekiel was built long ago and buried under massive amounts of dirt and rubble. I frankly expect that some will find the idea of a buried Temple hard to believe. I am only sharing these intriguing concepts

Ezekiel Tablets See page 3

The Amazing Ezekiel Tablets (continued)
Article by Dr. David A. Lewis (Page 3 of 3)

Ezekiel Tablets from page 2

with you because the information came to me, independently, from three different sources in Israel; also because Shlomo says it is tied in to the coded message of the stones.

Ezekiel's description of the Temple of the Messianic Era and the City of Jerusalem of that time describes great topographical changes. Jerusalem itself will become a great plain. Is it possible that the Ezekiel Temple, the Messianic Temple, is already in existence?

Jerusalem Courier and Prophecy Watch
Published by David Lewis Ministries, Inc.

David Allen Lewis, Publisher/Editor
Ramona Lewis, Business Manager
Dr. Stanley Horton, Advisor/Chaplain of Eschatology Club
Neil Howell, Consultant
Tom Brimmer, Jerusalem Correspondent
Becky Brimmer, Jerusalem Correspondent
Sandy Howell, Correspondent
Andrew Sands
Craig Valone, Assistant to Dr. Lewis
E. Dylan Hartsog, Volunteer - Technical Engineer, Computers, etc.
Chuck Heidle, Associate Evangelist/Co-host of Eschatology Club
Lee Fredrickson, Terry White, Design Editors
Armando Nuñez, Christians United for Israel (CUFI)-US Ambassador
Sherlock Bally, CUFI-International Ambassador
Aileen Ege, Volunteer
Mary Hitchcock, Volunteer
David ben Joseph Howell, Photographer, Writer
Mark Gentry, Chairman CUFI-Arkansas Chapter/USA Reporter

© 2006 by David A. Lewis Ministries, Inc.
You may request permission to reprint articles from the Prophecy Watch International or Jerusalem Courier. For articles we have reprinted contact original source. Please send copy of publication that material from David A. Lewis is quoted.

PO Box 14444, Springfield, MO 65814
Phone: 1-417-882-6470
Toll Free: 1-800-PSALM-87
Fax: 1-417-882-1135
Email: DALewMin@aol.com
Website: www.davidallenlewis.com

People who came to me . . . said that a bore hole had been dug and that some massive underground structure had been detected. What shall we say of these mysteries? Only time will tell.

Shlomo has explained to us about textual reasons indicating the originality of the Stones.

One of the textual clues is found in Ezekiel 1:2. Here is how the verse reads on the Stones: "In the fifth day of the month, which was the fifth year of Jehoiachin's captivity...." Here is the verse in the King James Version: "In the fifth day of the month, which was the fifth year of *King* Jehoiachin's captivity...." (same as the Masoretic Text). The word "king" does not appear on the stone tablets. The absence of word "king" shows that the author was familiar with King Jehoiachin, unlike the scribes that copied the Masoretic Text.

It seems that most, if not all, of the prophets felt their prophetic calling was an odious burden, not a thing to be desired. Think of Jeremiah, "I will not speak." Jonah refused to go to Ninevah. Isaiah cried out, "Woe is me." Amos complained that he had no desire to prophesy in the big city, preferring a bucolic, country life. It seems that only the prophet Ezekiel refrains from complaining about his calling.

On the Ezekiel Stones there is a Hebrew word that Shlomo translates, "He [God] cursed me." This could complete the register of protesting prophets. A very similar word in more recent Hebrew manuscripts, replaces the word on the stones giving a different meaning. With this Professor Stanley M. Horton, a great Hebrew scholar, agrees. Could this indicate an error on the part of the (later) scribe who copied the document?

The Hebrew on the stones is virtually identical to the Masoretic Text that today's Hebrew Bible is based upon. There are only slight scribal differences, such as the spelling of a word (by no means changing the meaning of the word). Compare the standard English translation of the Hebrew Bible with the King James version of the Original Covenant (OT) and you will be struck with the fact that they are virtually identical.

More details about the amazing discovery of the Ezekiel Tablets (how they got to Israel, current dwelling place, and secrets hidden in the text) can be found in chapter 6 "The Amazing Ezekiel Stones" of the book *Mysteries of the Bible Now Revealed*, edited by David A Lewis and Jim Combs. Dr Lewis also has made available a two-disk sermon set on "The Ezekiel Stones." These are available on Cassette and CD; please indicate your preference on the order form.

Visit our website today at www.davidallenlewis.com

Ezekiel Tablets Display
Jerusalem, Israel

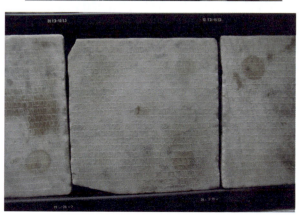

Excerpts from the Book - *Mother of the Pound:*
Memoirs on the Life and History of the Iraqi Jews
by David Kazzaz

Introduction - pg. 2

My people's long and proud history in what is now Iraq dates back some 2,500 years, to the Babylonian Exile of 586 BCE. At that time, the elite among the Jews of Israel were exiled by the god-king Nebuchadnezzar of Babylonia, who hoped to distance them from their First Temple and, ultimately, from the worship of God. The exiled Jews crossed the desert and proceeded to establish, under the spiritual leadership of the prophet Ezekiel, a thriving society in Babylonia, along the shores of the Euphrates River.

Fifty years later, Persia's King Cyrus came to rule over Babylonia and offered the Jews a chance to return to Israel and build their Second Temple. Those who stayed along the Euphrates and those who returned to their homeland established dual, vibrant Jewish centers in Babylon and in Jerusalem. But hard times lay ahead for both groups. The Jerusalemites would lose their Temple, while the Babylonians would have to contend with a number of invaders — some beneficent and some oppressive — over several centuries.

After Moslem Arabs arrived in the seventh century to rule Iraq and establish their capital in Baghdad, most of the Babylonian Jews moved from outlying areas and settled in the city. Depending on the whim of the Islamic ruler of the time, the Jewish community either flourished or retreated into a self-protective mode. The Mongols followed and brought good fortune to the Jews at one time, misfortune at another. The Turks came next, and their effect was also mixed.

Introduction - pg. 3

Many nations in their time of glory created vast empires by military conquest and included Jews as their subjects. However, these conquests did not force the Babylonian Jews to wander from place to place as other Jews would do over their long histories. Rather, the Babylonian Jews remained in one region for centuries and maintained their society with linear continuity. Consequently, they would be both the heirs and the guardians of traditions with deep and extensive roots. Perhaps this is why the spiritual aspects permeated and, indeed, defined so much of life in the Baghdad community of my youth.

Excerpts from the Book - *Mother of the Pound*

Holidays and Seasons - pg. 82

Pilgrimage

Shavuot, like all Jewish holidays, begins in the evening. Since this occasion celebrates the giving of the Ten Commandments, the first evening is spent reading biblical and rabbinic passages, prayers, and remembrances of the dead. In our house, all members of the extended family gathered together, each bringing candles to light for their dead ones, and the men took turns in the readings. Women prepared coffee and *meghli,* an herbal tea specially brewed for this occasion that children were allowed to drink and helped serve.

Holidays and Seasons - pg. 83

In Iraq during the 1930s, masses of Jewish people made the pilgrimage — not by foot but by car — to Kiffel, the burial place of our beloved prophet Ezekiel. Kiffel was a small town composed of mud houses and a few brick buildings, with narrow, serpentine dirt alleys meandering in-between. Most of the alleys led to the small river that coursed through the town, a tributary of the Euphrates. As religious pilgrims, our focal point in Kiffel was always Ezekiel's tomb, which was situated in a little domed building, part mud and part brick, with thick walls and only a few small windows. In front of the building was a large, open square that accommodated the many cars, carts, donkeys, and other modes of transportation. This space also served as an open market in which a wide variety of vendors randomly set up shop to sell all kinds of goods, from simple bedding to cooking utensils, food products, and a myriad of other items that the arriving pilgrims might need.

In the center of the burial building was a small, dark room

Excerpts from the Book - *Mother of the Pound*

Holidays and Seasons - pg. 83

containing Ezekiel's tomb. The tomb, some 8 feet long, 4 feet wide, and 6 feet high, was overlaid with several ornate covers on which Hebrew inscriptions from the Bible were embroidered. Only 6 or 8 feet separated the tomb from the walls of the room. When I visited this holy site, I was struck by the smell of wax that saturated the cool, damp air inside the building and the constantly changing patterns of light thrown off by the flickering candles.

In a custom shared by Jews and Moslems alike, all visitors to this dwelling took off their shoes before walking over the carpeted floor of the sacred room. As I entered the room, my ears caught the whispered prayers of fellow visitors. Each person would squeeze as close as possible to the tomb, kissing it and murmuring his or her prayers, petitions, and vows. The crowd moved slowly around the tomb in a counterclockwise manner. Others, most often men, stood at some distance from the tomb itself, reading psalms in hushed tones. (Something similar to our visit to Ezekiel's tomb can be experienced in Israel today at the building that shelters Rachel's tomb, on the road to Bethlehem.)

In the same building but outside Ezekiel's room, there were tombs of renowned rabbis who had died close to the time of the prophet's death, perhaps a century or two after the destruction of the First Temple in 586 BCE.

Holidays and Seasons - pg. 84

The pilgrims did not take offerings to God. They simply lit candles and beseeched the prophet Ezekiel to carry their wishes to God. They prayed, sang, and made true the commandment *"ve semachta ba chagecha"* (and you will bring joy to your holidays). The camping, the joy, and the spirit of celebration must have been similar to the festivities that were observed in Jerusalem, notwithstanding the lack of a temple and an offering.

So the Exile of the Babylonian Jews from Jerusalem did not really cause a disconnection after all, and the destruction of the Temple did not destroy the people. Defeat in the battle of Jerusalem did not ultimately vanquish the people who had fought so valiantly. To the contrary, Ezekiel and his inspiration helped the people to maintain and, indeed, even strengthen their connection to God and their faith; that was the secret of their survival.

Image of Nebuchadnezzar's dream

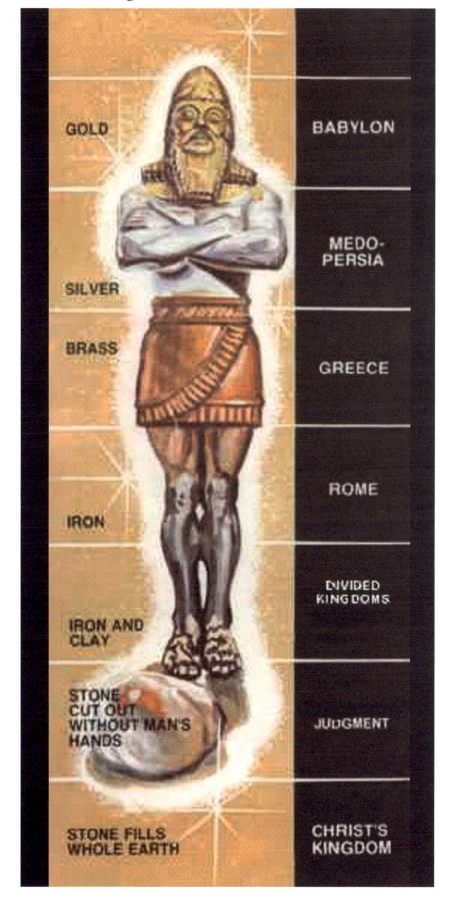

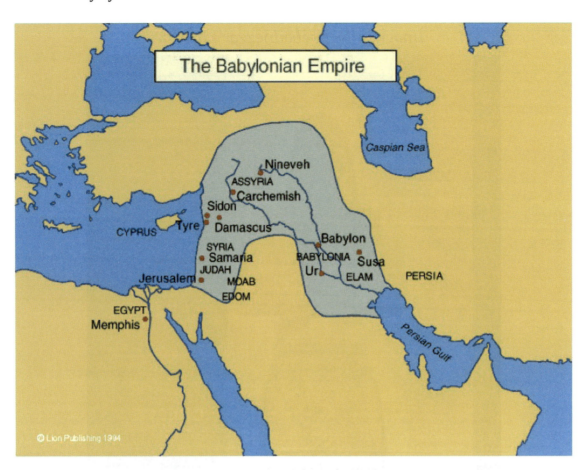
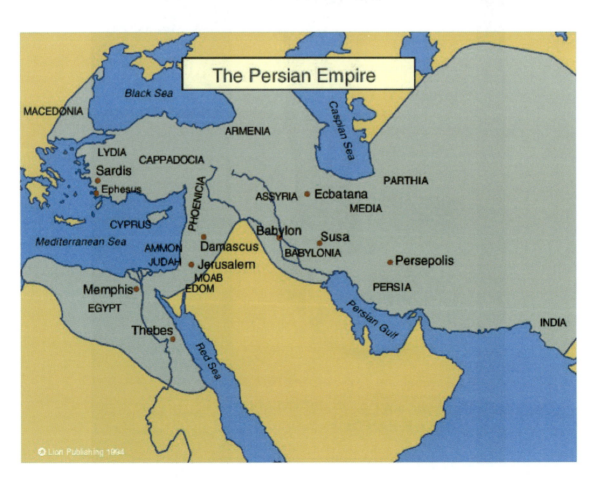

Quotes from, *The Wars of the Jews, Book VI*
by Flavius Josephus

Ch. 5, Pt. 2, pg. 582
...A false prophet was the occasion of these people's destruction, who had made a public proclamation in the city that very day, that God commanded them to get upon the temple, and that there they should receive miraculous signs of their deliverance. Now there was then a great number of false prophets suborned by the tyrants to impose on the people, who denounced this to them, that they should wait for deliverance from God;....

Ch. 5, Pt. 3, pg. 582
Thus were the miserable people persuaded by these deceivers, and such as belied God himself; while they did not attend nor give credit to the signs that were so evident, and did so plainly foretell their future desolation, but, like men infatuated, without either eyes to see or minds to consider, did not regard the denunciations that God made to them. Thus there was a star (20) resembling a sword, which stood over the city, and a comet, that continued a whole year. Thus also before the Jews' rebellion, and before those commotions which preceded the war, when the people were come in great crowds to the feast of unleavened bread, on the eighth day of the month Xanthicus, (21) [Nisan,] and at the ninth hour of the night, so great a light shone round the altar and the holy house, that it appeared to be bright day time; which lasted for half an hour. This light seemed to be a good sign to the unskillful, but was so interpreted by the sacred scribes, as to portend those events that followed immediately upon it. At the same festival also, a heifer, as she was led by the high priest to be sacrificed, brought forth a lamb in the midst of the temple. Moreover, the eastern gate of the inner (22) [court of the] temple, which was of brass, and vastly heavy, and had been with difficulty shut by twenty men, and rested upon a basis armed with iron, and had bolts fastened very deep into the firm floor, which was there made of one entire stone, was seen to be opened of its own accord about the sixth hour of the night. Now those that kept watch in the temple came hereupon running to the captain of the temple, and told him of it; who then came up thither, and not without great difficulty was able to shut the gate again. This also appeared to the vulgar to be a very happy prodigy, as if God did thereby open them the gate of happiness....

...for, before sun-setting, chariots and troops of soldiers in their armor were seen running about among the clouds, and surrounding of cities. Moreover, at that feast which we call Pentecost, as the priests were going by night into the inner [court of the temple,] as their custom was, to perform their sacred ministrations, they said that, in the first place, they felt a quaking, and heard a great noise, and after that they heard a sound as of a great multitude, saying, "Let us remove hence." But, what is still more terrible, there was one Jesus, the son of Ananus, a plebeian and a husbandman, who, four years before the war began, and at a time when the city was in very great peace and prosperity, came to that feast whereon it is our custom for every one to make tabernacles to God in the temple, (23) began on a sudden to cry aloud, "A voice from the east, a voice from the west, a voice from the four winds, a voice against Jerusalem and the holy house, a voice against the bridegrooms and the brides, and a voice against this whole people!" This was his cry, as he went about by day and by night, in all the lanes of the city....

Ch. 5, Pt. 3 continued, pg. 583
...This cry of his was the loudest at the festivals; and he continued this ditty for seven years and five months, without growing hoarse, or being tired therewith, until the very time that he saw his presage in earnest fulfilled in our siege, when it ceased;....

Ch. 5, Pt. 4, pg. 583
Now if any one consider these things, he will find that God takes care of mankind, and by all ways possible foreshows to our race what is for their preservation; but that men perish by those miseries which they madly and voluntarily bring upon themselves; for the Jews, by demolishing the tower of Antonia, had made their temple four-square, while at the same time they had it written in their sacred oracles, "That then should their city be taken, as well as their holy house, when once their temple should become four-square."...

Tyre, The Destruction of
(article from the internet, author unknown)

The Destruction of Tyre
In the year 595 B.C. a man named Ezekiel was given a prophecy regarding the city of Tyre, a city in the modern day country of Lebanon. At that time this city was a large thriving city and a great enemy of Israel. He was told:

> "Thus says the Lord God: "Behold I am against you O Tyre, and will cause many nations to come up against you, as the sea causes its waves to come up. And they shall destroy thewalls of Tyre and break down her towers; I will also scrape her dust from her and make her like the top of a rock. It shall be a place for the spreading of nets... It shall becomeplunder for the nations ... Behold I will bring against Tyre from the north King Nebuchadnezzer, King of Babylon... He will slay your people by the sword and your strong pillars will fall to the ground. They will plunder your riches and pillage your merchandise; they will break down your walls and destroy your pleasant houses; they will lay your stones, your timbers, and your soil in the midst of the water... I will make you like the top of a rock; you shall be a place for the spreading of nets, and you shall never be rebuilt, for I the Lord have spoken. Will the coast lands not shake at the sound of your fall ... Then all the princes of the sea will come down from their thrones, lay aside their robes, and take off their embroidered garments ... and be astonished at you."
> (Ezekiel 26:3)

These are the very specific prophecies for the city of Tyre made by a Hebrew prophet 2,600 years ago.

1. Nebuchadnezzer will destroy the mainland city of Tyre. (Ezekiel 26:8)
2. Many nations against Tyre. (Ezekiel 26:3)
3. Make her bare rock; flat like the top of a rock. (Ezekiel 26:4)
4. Fishermen will spread their nets over the site. (Ezekiel 26:5)
5. Throw the stones and timbers into the water. (Ezekiel 26:12)
6. Never be rebuilt. (Ezekiel 26:14)
7. Princes of nearby coast lands will be astonished by Tyre's fall and give up their thrones.

Now lets look at what secular history says happened to Tyre.

In the year 586 B.C. Nebuchadnezzer, the King of the Babylonian Empire began to attack the city of Tyre. The Babylonian army was the greatest fighting force up to that time and besieged the city of Tyre for 13 years. When they finally broke down the gates and walls of Tyre he found that the people had moved out to an island 1/2 mile off the coast of Tyre.

#1 fulfilled! City besieged.

Tyre, The Destruction of (article from the internet, author unknown) Continued

In the year 332 B.C. Alexander the Great laid siege against the island city of Tyre because they would not submit to his authority. The Encyclopedia Britannica states that because Alexander the Great had no fleet of ships he demolished old Tyre on the mainland and hethrew the debris (stones and timbers and dirt) into the ocean and made a causeway (jetty or wood/stone bridge) connecting the mainland to the newer island city of Tyre.

Secular historian Phillip Myers stated in his textbook of history that:
"Alexander the Great reduced Tyre to ruins in 332 B.C. Tyre recovered in a measure from this blow, but never regained the place she had previously held in the world. The larger part of the site of the once great city is now as bare as the top of a rock -- a place where the fishermen that still frequent the spot spread their nets to dry"!

#2, 3, 4, 5 fulfilled!

Secular historians have stated that the ruins of Tyre are highly unique. Tyre ruins are the only ones in the world that have been completely thrown into the ocean!

After Alexander the Great, the island city persisted in various degrees of strength. during the next 16 centuries. Many kings besieged the city until its final destruction by the Moslems began in 1291 A.D.

Currently, there is a flat rock area with not one stone upon another. The stones that were thrown into the sea are still there. Other than a few nearby small fishing villages, there is no evidence of the former great city. On the flat former foundation stones you find to the present day fishermen drying their nets!

#6 fulfilled! Never rebuilt.

Secular historians record that when Alexander the Great besieged the city of Tyre thatmany of the neighboring kings submitted to his authority without a battle.

#7 fulfilled! Princes give up their thrones.

The Seat of Satan
by Dr. Billye Brim

Rev. 2:12 and to the angel of the church in Pergamum write: These things saith he that hath the sharp two-edged sword:
Rev. 2:13 I know where thou dwellest, even where Satan's throne is; and thou holdest fast my name, and didst not deny my faith, even in the days of Antipas my witness, my faithful one, who was killed among you, where Satan dwelleth (sits). (ASV)

One day as I crossed The Rhema Bible Training Center campus in Tulsa, Patsy Behrman (now Camaneti) called me to the prayer room to pray with a young couple who felt called to Brussels. As we prayed, we were overcome—in a wonderful way—by the power of God. Soon after I received an invitation to accompany them to Brussels for a prayer conference they were calling "Breakthrough for Brussels."

On March 25, 1991, I walked down to the water's edge from my home on a bluff overlooking a lake near Pryor, Oklahoma. Seated on a rock in a secluded place, I began to pray about whether I should go.

Immediately the Lord spoke to me. He unveiled strategies of Satan and his seats (thrones) of rule from what I will call the mid-heavens, or the double kingdom system set up after Adam allowed the adversary a place in this world.

The Double Kingdom System

In Ezekiel 28, the Lord directs His message to a human earthly ruler, *the prince of Tyre.* He says, "Thou art a man" (v. 2).

But then, starting in verse 11, He addresses one as *the King of Tyre.* This one is identified as having been in Eden, an anointed cherub who had been upon the holy mountain of God—a created being (Ez. 28:13-15).

This reveals how the double-kingdom system operates; an evil spirit in the heavenlies influences an earthly ruler, a man. Satan, called "the king of Tyre," ruled down through the earthly ruler called "the prince of Tyre."

Satan used the royal family of Tyre to oppose the plan of God for the Jews. Jezebel was of that family. She married the king of Israel and brought with her prophets of Baal.

Daniel, who'd been carried off to Babylon just before the fall of the Temple, saw prophecy coming to pass. The Bible states that, "In the third year of Cyrus king of Persia…" Daniel fasted and prayed for three weeks" (Dan. 10:1-3).

What the angel said when he came with the answer enlightens us about the double kingdom system:

Dan. 10:12 Then he said to me, "Do not be afraid, Daniel, for from the first day that you set your heart on understanding *this* and on humbling yourself before your God, your words were heard, and I have come in response to your words.
Dan. 10:13 "But the prince of the kingdom of Persia was withstanding me for twenty-one days; then behold, Michael, one of the chief princes, came to help me, for I had been left there with the *kings of Persia.* (ASV)

After delivering the message, the angel refers again to the evil spirits in the heavenlies:

> **Dan. 10:20** Then he said, "Do you understand why I came to you? But I shall now return to fight against the prince of Persia; so I am going forth, and behold, the prince of Greece is about to come. (ASV)

Persia (present day Iran) then ruled over the captive children of Israel. It was through the Persian kingdom the evil Haman attempted to wipe out the Jews. God destroyed Haman through Esther and Mordechai. When Daniel prayed, God's prophecy concerning Cyrus' helping the Jews return home was challenged. Satan, who had set up a throne over Persia, attempted to thwart God's plans for Israel.

Lucifer Lusts After the Throne of God

Lucifer was created an anointed angel. He made a devil out of himself. We are told how it happened.

Satan's throne is not now in hell. The Bible calls him, *the prince of the powers of the air* (Eph. 2:2). He has set up his headquarters in the mid-heavens. This place of rule was intended for Adam. The first man, legally, but not morally, delivered the operations from the heavenlies to Satan.

John A. MacMillan writes in *The Authority of the Believer* (page 10):

> [It] is commonly understood by those who carefully study the Word, that the kingdoms of this world are under the control and leadership of satanic principalities. The great head of these is...acknowledged as the "prince of this world" by our Lord Himself (John 12:31). His [Satan's] asserted claim to the suzerainty of the world kingdoms, made in the presence of the Lord Jesus (Luke 4:6) was not denied by Christ. Although a rebel against the Most High and now under judgment, of dispossession, he is still at large, and as the masses of mankind are also rebels, he maintains over them an unquestioned, because unsuspected rule, their eyes being blinded to his dominance (2 Cor. 4:4).

When Satan does at last descend into hell, the kings of the earth who followed him during their reigns will ask him, "How art thou fallen from heaven, O Lucifer, son of the morning! How art thou cut down to the ground which didst weaken the nations!" (Is. 14:12).

Then comes God's answer, "For thou hast said in thine heart, I will ascend into heaven, I will exalt my throne above the stars of God: I will sit also upon the mount of the congregation in the sides of the north; I will ascend above the heights of the clouds; I will be like the most High. Yet thou shall be brought down to hell, to the sides of the pit"
(Is. 14:13-15).

Lucifer had a throne. It was in a place that required ascending to approach heaven. It was in a place that had clouds. It was on earth in the pre-Adamic civilization. (See my book, *The Blood and the Glory*.) Lucifer led an attack on Heaven with the goal of setting up his throne on God's Holy Mountain in Heaven.

Jesus told us how it turned out, *"I beheld Satan as lightning fall from Heaven"* (Luke 10:18).

The Seat of Satan at Pergamon

As I sat on that rock beside Lake Hudson in Oklahoma, the Lord reminded me of what Jesus said to the angel of the church at Pergamon. (See Scripture above.)

The Lord showed me that Satan moves his throne from place to place — and that history reflects it.

> <u>Bullinger's note in *The Companion Bible*</u>
> "Pergamos. A city in Mysia famous for the worship of Aesculapius, to whom the title soter (saviour) was given and whose emblem was the serpent...Some trace the Babylonian pagan priesthood as removing to Pergamos."

The Lord made known to me that at the time of Jesus' appearing to John on the Isle of Patmos, Satan had set up his throne over Pergamon. Pagan cults and emperor worship were centered there. The huge Altar of Zeus dominated the acropolis over the ancient Greek city in what is now Turkey.

The Lord made known to my spirit that Satan had since set up his throne over Berlin in World Wars I and II. And that his throne was over Moscow during the Cold War.

I heard in my spirit, *The adversary will set up his throne over Brussels before he attempts the move to Jerusalem where he plans to set himself up in the rebuilt Temple* (Dan. 9:27; Matt. 24:15; 2 Thess. 2:3, 4). *I want you in Brussels as my witness.*

So for years I have been going to Brussels in my ministry as a witness (Acts 26:16).

The Lord has since made me to know that earthly Jerusalem is not Satan's final goal. He plans another attempt to ascend to the heavenly Jerusalem and the throne of God. How wonderful to read the Book of Revelation and the utter frustration of the plans of the enemy in the judgments of God.

Tracing the Moves

Eerily there has been a physical counterpart—*an earthly reflection of the seat of Satan in the heavenlies*—in each of the cities the Lord pointed out to me. That counterpart is a huge structure. Yet in modern times it has moved from ancient Pergamon to Berlin. From Berlin to Moscow. And then back to Berlin where it now sits.

Here is the story of the seemingly impossible travels of such a gargantuan structure, the great Pergamon Altar of Zeus.

The New German Empire began in 1871. Associations were made with the Ottoman Empire of Turkey. A German road builder who was also an archeologist, discovered the ruins of Pergamon and the Altar of Zeus. Kaiser Wilhelm became passionately involved with transporting the huge altar to Berlin. And there it stood in a specially constructed museum during World War I.

Hitler was enamored with the altar and some say, worshiped at it. In 1934 he ordered the building of a sports field in Nuremberg patterned after the altar. Here huge Nazi rallies with swastika-emblazoned-flags were staged in cultish array. Hitler spoke from the altar-like edifice. All during the Nazi reign of horror the altar stood in their capital.

U.S. General George Patton led the allied armies in the final land thrust resulting in the taking of Berlin. Under orders, the U.S. led forces stepped back to allow Russia to actually take the city because of the Nazi siege of Leningrad. This step, however, led to the dividing of Berlin during the Cold War and the building of the Berlin Wall. Guess on which side of the wall the Pergamon Museum stood! It stood in Communist East Berlin. However, the altar itself was dismantled and taken to Moscow.

> The massive Pergamon Altar, originally removed from the Greek city of Pergamon to Germany, was dismembered, carefully packed and sent to Moscow in 1945...the Russians discovered it hidden [imagine hiding something that large] by the Germans in the Zoo tower in Berlin which was supposed to be bomb proof. The Zoo tower contained crates of art treasures stolen by the Germans from victims during the Allied bombings.
> ("THE TRAIL OF PAINT - The Nazi Art Obsession" by Phyllis Farber, April 1998).

Some years before the actual transportation of the altar to Moscow, however, the Soviet architect Alexey Schusev designed Lenin's tomb using the altar of Zeus as his pattern. During the height of Communism the Soviet leaders stood atop the tomb as the power of the Russian Communist army and artillery paraded before them in a fashion memorable of the Nazi parades in Hitler's Nuremberg arena.

In 1957 the altar itself returned to Berlin—the capital of one of the two powerful states (Germany and France) which drive the European Union.

The entrance to the strange building, *The Palais de Justice* in Brussels, built by Leopold II and the architect Pouilart, bears a remarkable resemblance to the altar of Zeus. It was the largest building in the Western Hemisphere when it was built between 1866-1883. Conglomerations of architectural design from the Four Empires of the Times of the Gentiles from the Book of Daniel are used in the huge structure. Stairways and passages, which go nowhere, add to the eeriness of the building. The architect was declared mad.

We Saw the Seat of Satan

In the summer of 2003, four of us traveled to Berlin to see the Pergamon Museum. The size of the Altar of Zeus is as staggering as its history. Then too, it is housed alongside another ancient artifact the Germany also transported into its kingdom—the Ishtar Gates of Babylon. The Ishtar Gates and their passageway, through which the children of Israel entered captive into Babylon, stand like a tribute to those who captured the Chosen People.

Study Syllabus for
The Book of Ezekiel

Sources

Archbold, Norma. *The Mountains of Israel: The Bible and the West Bank.* ISBN 965-90100-01. Single copies: Amazon.com. For resale: Email for 800 number - npabooks@comcast.net.

Baron, David. *ZECHARIAH, A Commentary on his Visions and Prophecies.* Grand Rapids, MI. Kregal.

Editors: Scherman, Rabbi Nosson, Zlotowitz, Rabbi Meir. *Trei Asar, The Twelve Prophets, Vol. 1: Hosea, Joel, Amos, Obadiah,* ArtScrolls Tanach Series. Brooklyn, NY. Mesorah Publications, Ltd.

Ibid. *The Chumash, The Stone Edition.*

Hagin, Kenneth E. *Marriage, Divorce & Remarriage.* Tulsa, OK. 2001, 2006.

Pearleman, Myer, *Through the Bible Book by Book,* Gospel Publishing House, Springfield, MO

BIBLES
American Standard Version (1901)

The Companion Bible. With Notes and Appendixes by E. W. Bullinger. Kregal Publications, Grand Rapids, MI.

God's Word Translation

The Numerical Bible, Loizeaux Brothers, Neptune, N.J., Commentary by Samuel Rideout and F. W. Grant. 1932.

Yechezkel, ArtScroll Tanach Series, Mesorah Publications, Ltd. Brooklyn, NY. 2007.

Young's Literal Translation